God's Wonderful Family

Growing up as Sons

By

Roger Price

NEW WINE PRESS

New Wine Press
PO Box 17
Chichester PO20
England

First published by New Wine Press in 1986
ISBN 00 947852 19 0

Printed and bound in Great Britain by
Anchor Brendon Ltd, Tiptree, Essex

Dedication

I dedicate this book to Derrick and Thelma Reeks who through the 'Rivers of Life' conferences, organized between 1978–1984, blessed so many people in the Body of Christ. For myself I recognize and thank them for the invaluable role they played in the expansion of my own ministry during that time.

Acknowledgements

Writing a book is never easy, but the task is helped so much by constant encouragement. My wife, Ros, is always a source of inspiration and has often revived my flagging spirit.

Pam Melia, so diligent in typing this manuscript, has often gone 'the extra mile', and while under no obligation at all to encourage, has done so constantly. I am indebted to her.

I owe thanks too to Malcolm Coulson who, willing and uncomplaining as ever, pored over the manuscript and, together with my wife, removed the rough edges and awkward corners.

Without the Lord Jesus Christ, who saved me and washed me from my sins, this book could not have been written at all. My most grateful thanks go to Him.

Foreword

The relationships that exist between Christian people, and with God Himself, are represented to us in many ways, but it was Jesus Himself who taught us to use the name 'Father' and who called his followers 'brothers and sisters'. The family of God is not simply a way of thinking about His followers, a simile with the human family as its starting point. Rather, His family is the pattern for our life on earth, disrupted or distorted as that may often be. And if the family is His creation, what is its purpose and potential for the whole man, and particularly for those who know Him as Father?

In this book Roger Price has outlined God's purposes in the institution that is the foundation of our individual existence, as well as of our relationships with one another. His invigorating discussion owes little to sociology or anthropology; instead, he draws upon the Scriptures for an understanding that will not only help the individual believer, but also will strengthen and refresh Christian family life. I warmly commend it.

Ian Lodge Patch

Contents

Introduction

For some time my children found it very confusing that while others called me Mr Price, Roger or Uncle Roger, they had to stick to the names 'Dad' or 'Daddy'. Their mother called me 'Darling' and would only use 'Roger' if she was trying to catch my attention, or was speaking about me to someone else. It was mysterious to them, because they hadn't realised that in the closeness of a family, proper names tend to be dropped, and are replaced with terms of affection.

When we look at the Bible with this in mind we begin to see something most remarkable; that our God is addressed in just the sort of terms which apply in a family. Nowhere are we told his personal name – the Bible is silent on that – although we are told many things about Him. From His titles alone, for instance, we learn that He is 'The Almighty God', 'The Lord of Hosts', 'The Everlasting God', 'The Lord that heals', 'The Lord our Peace' and so on, but never His actual name.

Instead we are constantly told and encouraged to call Him 'Father'. Many of us have grown so accustomed to this, that it comes as something of a shock to be told that it is not true of any other major religion. Ra, Vishnu, Amon, Zeus, Aphrodite – the list of names goes on and on – but never are their followers allowed to call them 'father'. The

Muslim, for example, has 99 names for 'Allah' but 'Father' is not among them!

It is no surprise therefore to learn that the God of the Bible isn't a distant, angry, isolated Being like the named gods. He is a God who delights in being the Head of a wonderful family, whose children can approach Him with boldness and freedom whenever they want. He is a God of Love who cares for them, who has provided all they need to ensure that they will be with Him forever, and who positively delights in them.

This affects all His dealings with us. Just how is best illustrated by the well-known, but apocryphal, story of a judge in a certain country who found himself presiding over a trial in which his own son was in the dock. At the end of the trial the man found his son guilty and fined him heavily. He then came down from the bench, took out his cheque book and paid the fine himself. Then he took the boy home to deal with him privately!

Such a thing would not, of course, be allowed and yet it is exactly the situation God is said to be in with us. The Bible shows God as a Judge; yet not a Judge only, but a loving father too. Oh what a difference that makes.

Out Father has found us guilty, and pronounced us sinners; but He has also sent His own Son into the world to pay the price for our sin. 'God made him who had no sin to be sin for us, so that in him we might become the righteousness of God' (2 Cor. 5:21 NIV). His sacrifice has availed for us.

Such love is too wonderful for us to grasp fully, but what it means is that, for us who believe and who are therefore His children, God is Someone who cares deeply, and undertakes to provide for all our needs.

1. I am grateful to John Gilchrist for his booklet 'The Love of God in the Quran and the Bible'. Christianity and Islam Series Number 7. F.F.M. Publications.

The purpose of this book is to show how God's Fatherhood has changed everything in the lives of us, His children, and to show something of what it means to bear the name 'Sons of God'.

May God use it in leading us all into a revelation of His love, that we may . . . 'behold what manner of love the Father has bestowed upon us, that we should be called the sons of God' (1 John 3:1).

1

Father Loves Me

The love that God had for me was the biggest surprise I had ever received. It came bursting into my unhappy life on that November day in 1965 and swept me off my feet.

'But it can't be that simple – and you can't be that foolish' had been my usual scathing response when the Christians had told me of their conversions. To suggest that God, if He existed at all, could be *that* real and would be able let alone *willing*, to intervene in a person's life had always struck me as utterly ridiculous. Surely these people had been brainwashed or had convinced themselves. Perhaps they needed a feeling of security and had invented 'God' so that they could feel that SOMEONE out there was really in control in this chaos. God surely only made sense to those who couldn't face reality.

Yet there was something really different about them. It wasn't just that they spoke about God and Jesus as if they were real; they had an inner glow in their lives, a tranquillity which was utterly alien to me, and a smile on their faces that said 'I'm a thoroughly loved person'.

I knew I didn't like them; they made me feel uncomfortable. They had something and that something was what I and those around me were seeking and yet pretending to have.

Jesus had told his disciples to be 'as wise as serpents'

and when one of the 'God Squad' invited me to attend a meeting so that I could debate the issues with the speaker, I didn't know just how cunning and serpentine he was being. I didn't know that God was eagerly anticipating the birth of another child.

I had gone equipped to the meeting and I thought I was ready for anything. My bible in those days was Bertrand Russell's booklet 'Why I am not a Christian' and I had read it again and again to be ready for anything. However my 'anything' hadn't included the inner conviction of the Holy Spirit.

Harold Owen's[1] sparkling eyes seemed to encompass the whole group of us and I sat in the furthest and darkest corner trying to avoid his gaze. It was announced that he would speak for 45 minutes and then answer any questions we wanted to put to him. Within five minutes I was regretting going to the meeting. Something inside me was stirring and disturbing me and I was not able to concentrate on anything else. Why had I come? I couldn't really hear what the speaker was saying anyway; all I knew was that I couldn't ignore my unhappy loneliness and my utter sinfulness any more. The talk seemed to last for eternity and how I kept my place I do not know. All I remember is that as I ran from the room someone was asking 'Any questions, anybody?'

The darkness of my own room, which had been so soothing in the past, did nothing this time to calm my inner turmoil. I had been busy filling my time for years trying to cut out my distress and need. Now it came crashing in upon me. I couldn't pretend any more.

Could it just be that God WAS real and that He really did care? All logic seemed against it, and yet those Christians were immovable in their belief that it was so. It

1. Harold Owen is now Pastor of 'The Coyne' in Woking.

wasn't just words either; their lives showed a release and lightness which seemed to shout 'my sins are forgiven, my burden is gone'.

I knew it was time for reality. My way didn't work for me, let alone anyone else – it hadn't given me peace and assurance. I couldn't face my failure, my sins or my future; I felt old before my time; I was sceptical about life itself and had a sneaking feeling that the golden promise of youth would soon evaporate into a fatalistic acceptance of my lot, and eventual disillusionment and a sense of futility. Hadn't the optimistic, life-loving Mark Twain ended his life in that way? Before he died he wrote 'A myriad of men are born. They labour, sweat and struggle for bread; they squabble and scold and fight; they scrabble for little mean advantages over each other. Age creeps upon them; infirmities follow; shames and humiliations bringing down their prides and their vanities; those they love are taken from them and the joy of life is turned into aching grief; the burden of pain and care and misery grows heavier year by year; at length ambition is dead, pride is dead, vanity is dead, longing for relief is in their place. It comes at last – Death, the only unpoisoned gift Earth ever had for them and they vanish from a world where they were of no consequence, where they achieved nothing; where they were a mistake and a failure and a foolishness, where they have left no sign that they existed – a world which will lament them for a day and forget them forever. Then another myriad takes their place and copies all they did and goes along the same profitless road and vanishes as they vanished to make room for another and another – millions of myriads to follow the same arid path, through the same desert and accomplish what the first myriad and all the other myriads which came after it accomplished – NOTHING'. Was this to be my lot also?

In that darkened room (no 317) I sat with my eyes wide open and prayed. A simple, proud, agnostic yet genuine prayer: 'God if you exist (and I don't really know that you do) I want you to know that I need you, and if you will prove yourself to me, to my own intellectual satisfaction (!!), I promise I will give you my life.'

I expected nothing and received everything. The dynamic personality of the resurrected Jesus filled the room and an invisible light seemed to penetrate the former darkened gloom. Tears of sheer joy burst out of my eyes and cascaded down my cheeks. I had cried often before, usually late at night and usually about my mother who had died fourteen years before. This was different – the tears that flowed were like streams in the desert, tears of laughter, happiness and sheer relief. I just knew that Jesus was the Saviour of the World, that He was alive and at that moment – most important of all – that I was loved by God Himself. Such knowledge was too great for me to take in, yet I knew it intuitively.

Two hours later as I was rushing across the University Campus to tell my friends what had happened to me I sang the only song I could think of – a worldly song called 'For once in my life I've got someone who loves me.' I have often wondered since what a spectator would have made of it all – a thin, dark student running through the night, tears streaming down his now beaming, smiling face and singing at the top of his voice! Not all Welshmen sing in tune, either. Not that I cared – the love of God had captivated and transformed me. That 'God so loved the world that He gave His one and only Son, that whoever believes in him shall not perish but have eternal life' (John 3:16 NIV), wasn't a debating point any more; it had left the realms of dusty theology and become a pulsating reality, the greatest and most important fact of my whole life. I was born again, a new creation and a child of God. I was so unused to smiling that my cheeks ached for weeks after and I had to massage them!

I was later to learn to my amazement that the joy I experienced on that night, twenty years ago, was but a poor reflection of the joy and rejoicing that had occurred in heaven on that same night. Jesus surprised hard-hearted Pharisees and Scribes who objected to his eating with sinners by saying 'I tell you, there is rejoicing in the presence of the angels of God over one sinner who repents' (Luke 15:10 NIV).

It is easy to assume that this verse simply teaches the undoubtedly correct fact that God's angels take a deep interest in our salvation. In fact, however, the truth it contains far transcends that; it is that the God who dwells in the presence of the angels and who sits on a throne surrounded by them is Himself the One who seeks sinners and who rejoices with unutterable joy when one repents. God the Father had been thrilled with my conversion.

The prophet Zephaniah foresaw this: 'The Lord your God is with you, he is mighty to save. He will take great delight in you . . . he will rejoice over you with singing' (Zeph. 3:17 NIV).

Such knowledge is difficult for us to grasp, but grasp it we must. We have got to know how much God loves us and be able to walk through our lives, down the often bumpy highways, with our heads held high and with the glint in our eye that tells the world that we are the redeemed of the Lord, the children of God on whom He has set His love. Paul expresses how vital it is when in Ephesians 3:17-19 (NIV) he prays 'that you, being rooted and established in love, may have power, together with all the saints, to grasp how wide and long and high and deep is the love of Christ, and to know this love that surpasses knowledge – that you may be filled to the measure of all the fulness of God.'

17

How God's heart must ache when He sees His children oppressed and heavy because they have failed to see the love He has for them.

I still remember the picture that once came to my mind as I was studying Luke 15:10. It was of my Father in heaven looking over the edge of a cloud and pointing so that all the angels of heaven knew who He was talking about and He was saying 'That's my boy down there.' And He meant me! The dark valley of my lovelessness was transformed into a mountain overflowing with love at the very thought. I cannot forget the look on His face. It was the look which appears on the face of every father as the birth of his child is announced. To be 'made in the image of god' encompasses more than we could ever have dreamed and men simply reflect what God Himself feels over every one of us who has been born from above.

All of us need to see that look in God's face and know it is us He has in mind. Only then will we know how much He loves us, and how precious we are.

The same truth is behind the parable of the merchant seeking pearls. Matthew 13:45-46 (NIV) tells the tale. 'Again, the kingdom of heaven is like a merchant looking for fine pearls. When he found one of great value, he went away and sold everything he had and bought it.'

I have never been convinced or satisfied by the explanation which identifies the merchant of the story as the sinner seeking God. Upon finding the truth he or she then apparently sells all to gain it. When I thought of myself as the merchant I asked 'what was it that I had sold to gain Jesus?' All I could think of was my depression, despair, guilt and lots of other horrible things. They weren't saleable riches. It was nonsensical – it amounted to giving up a life of degradation, no more and no less.

If that interpretation is wrong then it leaves only one alternative – an alternative so beautiful and amazing that at first we dare not consider it. If we are not the merchant, then we must be the pearl!

Who then is the merchant? It has to be God Himself. The Lord of heaven, so loving us, that when He found us He even gave His only Son, who in turn left heaven's glory and humbled Himself, enduring death by crucifixion that He might gain us. Oh what love, sacrifice and suffering is contained in the simple statement that 'Jesus Christ came into the world to save sinners' (1 Tim. 1:15 NIV). No wonder the slave trader John Newton poured himself out in adoration and penned 'Amazing love, how can it be that Thou my God should die for me?'

This parable alone shows us the depth of God's love and the lengths to which He went to gain us, and at the same time shows to every one of us just how precious we are in His sight. 'You see, at just the right time, when we were still powerless, Christ died for the ungodly. Very rarely will anyone die for a righteous man, though for a good man someone might possibly dare to die. But God demonstrates His own love for us in this: While we were still sinners, Christ died for us' (Rom 5:6-8 NIV).

Never again let us think of ourselves as worthless – God has bought us with a price, not with pounds or dollars or silver or gold, 'but with the precious blood of Christ, a lamb without blemish or defect' (1 Peter 1:19 NIV). What I am prepared to pay for anything shows the value I put upon it and the price God paid for you shows your true worth in His sight.

Sitting perched on top of the Pennines, halfway between Newcastle-upon-Tyne and the Lake District is the market town of Alston. In one of its main streets is an old bottle shop on whose shelves are found just about every type, shape and colour of bottle. Apparently many bottle collectors make the long journey to Alston to try and add some precious piece to their collection. Every bottle carries a little tag with a price on it. As a non-collector of bottles some of the prices staggered me, but the owner assured me that many who came to his shop counted bottles so precious they were prepared to pay far higher than the £20 or so that he was asking.

Our God counted us so precious that He was prepared to see His own Son's blood shed in payment for us. It is the blood which constantly reminds us of our preciousness and fully shows us the mind of God towards us. When the enemy creeps around and whispers in our ears that we are useless, worthless good-for-nothings we can literally do as the believers of the book of Revelations will do, that is overcome him 'by the blood of the lamb and by the word of their testimony' (Rev. 12:11 NIV). On such occasions we must remind him of the price God has paid for us, for that is our true worth. The devil and the world may reject us and scorn us, but God counts us precious.

No wonder an American friend of mine, whose Germanic background had left her with the surname Junk, decided when she became a Christian that she just had to change her name. She had it legally altered to acknowledge the work God had wrought in her life. No more is she Miss Junk, but now Miss Suzanna Worth! Hallelujah. We all need her revelation.

What God said to Israel of old, He says to us today: 'They shall be mine, saith the Lord of hosts, in that day when I make up my jewels' (Malachi 3:17). What a variety and abundance there will be too, for our God is a creator and collector of jewels.

A study of the Old Testament shows quite clearly that representing His people as precious stones is a feature of God's design. The breastplate of the High Priest of Israel contained twelve precious stones, each one of which represented a tribe.

We read of its design in Exodus 28: 17-21 'And thou

shalt set in it settings of stones, even four rows of stones: the first row shall be a sardius, a topaz, and a carbuncle: this shall be the first row. And the second row shall be an emerald, a sapphire, and a diamond. And the third row a ligure, an agate and an amethyst. And the fourth row a beryl, and an onynx, and a jasper: they shall be set in gold in their inclosings. And the stones shall be with the names of the children of Israel, twelve, according to their names, like the engravings of a signet; every one with his name shall they be according to the twelve tribes (KJV).

The pairing[1] is as follows:

Sardius = Judah	Topaz = Issachar	Crbuncle = Zebulun
Emerald = Reuben	Sapphire = Simeon	Diamond = Gad
Ligure = Ephraim	Agate = Manasseh	Amethyst = Benjamin
Beryl = Dan	Onyx = Asher	Jasper = Naphtali

The relationship between the stones and the tribes is not haphazard but shows a definite connection between the character of the tribe and the nature of the stone. Reuben was an unstable individual, as unstable as the sea, and his stone, the emerald, was sea-green. Simeon was represented as a sapphire – the second hardest stone in the world. Just as it could scratch and tear, so he was hard and tore a community to shreds. He is classed together with his vicious brother Levi. Judah's stone was the ruby red stone called in the KJV 'a sardius'. From his tribe would come the Saviour of the world. And so we could go on. There is a parallel between each precious stone and tribe.

So what is the message in the fact that the Church and every individual member of it, is represented by a pearl in the parable in Matthew 13? Why, we must ask, did God sovereignly choose a pearl?

1. C. W. Slemming agrees with this pairing in his book 'These are the Garments'. Christian Literature Crusade.

Undoubtedly the way in which a pearl is formed mirrors the formation of the Church. Unlike the hard resistant gems which are formed in the pressurized boiling chasms of the Earth, a pearl can only exist where there has been suffering. It isn't the mighty volcanic convulsions which produce a pearl, but the agony of an oyster trying to rid itself of the irritation of a piece of sand or grit. A more contrasting mode of creation would be hard to imagine, and yet among the precious jewels the pearl alone comes from such living suffering.

We too trace our spiritual birth to living suffering. We do not come from a direct creative act of an angry God but from the sacrifice of Christ who was led as a lamb – the meekest of animals – to the slaughter. Our new birth finds its roots in His passion.

But what is it that causes God to see a similarity between us and a pearl? First of all must be the sheer preciousness of the pearl. The ancient historian Pliny[2] described pearls as 'the richest merchandise of all, and the most sovereign commodity in the whole world.' In Rome itself only those of highest rank were permitted to wear them. We, who are Christians, have in the same way been bought with the highest price by the only One who is truly worthy, the King of Kings and Lord of Lords.

Secondly, unlike diamonds, sapphires and the other jewels, pearls are very delicate and soft and need special care and handling. No pane of glass was ever etched by a pearl. They can be scratched by a pin or a coin; friction with most fabrics can remove their lustre and the slight acidity of rain water or perspiration can do them untold damage and cause them to decompose.

As a result of this pearls are usually set into gold or silver in brooches or earrings, or worn on silk. The Queen

2. Quoted from 'Encyclopaedia Britannica' Vol. 17.

has a picture of her father and grandfather set in pearls and wears them on pieces of pink and turquoise silk pinned to the left side of her dress. Should anyone wear them directly on their skin it is for a limited time only and they are carefully bathed afterwards. They need constant care and attention.

We are designed to be soft like that too. Often our experiences in the world and the tragedies of our lives have caused us to be hard and self-protective, but that isn't God's plan for us. God has removed our hard stony hearts and replaced them at salvation with soft hearts of flesh. He does not want us as iron or diamond but as a pearl, and knowing our softness and weakness He has set us in a firm foundation, and has entered into an eternal covenant of care with us. 'We are the people of His pasture, and the sheep of his hand' (Psalm 95:7).

Not only has He set our feet upon a rock, and hidden us in the cleft of the rock, but we are also 'rooted and established in love' (Eph. 3:17 NIV) and from these most precious settings our beauty can be seen.

Paul writes in Ephesians 5:25-27 (NIV) 'Husbands, love your wives, just as Christ loved the church and gave himself up for her to make her holy, cleansing her by the washing with water through the word, and to present her to himself as a radiant church, without stain or wrinkle or any other blemish . . . . ' And later in verse 29 he continues 'no one ever hated his own body, but he feeds and cares for it, just as Christ does the church – for we are members of His body.' He nourishes and cherishes us and sets us in His love so that we can show forth the peace, love and joy which He has poured upon us with such abundance. He is our fortress and shield.

'The battle is the Lord's' (1 Samuel 17:47 NIV); 'Do not be afraid. Stand firm and you will see the deliverance the Lord will bring you today. . . . The Lord will fight for

you; you need only be still' (Exodus 14:13 and 14 NIV);
'So do not fear, for I am with you; do not be dismayed, for
I am your God. I will strengthen you and help you; I will
uphold you with my righteous right hand' (Isaiah 41:10
NIV). 'For I, saith the Lord, will be unto her a wall of fire
round about. . . . for he that toucheth you toucheth the
apple of his eye[3]' (Zech. 2:5 and 8).

What more proof do we need of His covenant of care?
He is our champion, our kinsman-redeemer and we can
relax under the shadow of His wings.

Last of all a pearl is iridescent and translucent – it is
designed to sparkle and glow. So are we to let the life and
light of Jesus be seen in us.

As Father saw the universe and its treasures spread
before Him, what more fitting and perfect jewel could He
choose? The pearl expressed all He wanted to say.

He loves us, He cares for us – we are beautiful and soft
in His sight. More than that He gave His very heart that
He might have us.

A duo in Carlisle sings a song which expresses it all
perfectly.

> 'The Lord loves me,
> And, oh, the wonder I see.
> A rainbow shines through my window
> The Lord loves me.'[4]

Amen and Amen

---

3. Lit 'the pupil of my eye'. It is a medical fact that the eye is the most
protected part of the human body having at least five protective
mechanisms. How many more are at work in our lives?
4. It is sung to the tune 'Plaisir D'Amour'. I have been unable to
establish the copyright of the words.

2

Our Father in Heaven

The benefits of our salvation dawned slowly upon me. At first the only thing that mattered was that God loved me and that my sinfulness and failure were no longer a barrier between us, but as time went on, the full length and breadth of all that God had done surprised and delighted me.

I belonged. The group which I had disliked so intensely now became my daily companions and I knew that they accepted me unconditionally – as Oliver Cromwell said – 'Warts and all'. In the Psalms David wrote 'God sets the lonely in families, He leads forth the prisoners with singing' (Psalm 68:6 NIV), and it was my delight in the months and years following my conversion to discover both these in full measure.

I had never understood why Christians had so often been referred to as 'brethren' or 'brothers and sisters'. Now, with a revelation of God as my own Father, I could understand. Not only had God saved us, He had caused us to become members of His own family, children by birth and therefore related through Him to one another. Clearly God was our Father and we were His family.

The family is very important to God and it is one of the highest expressions of His love. 1 John 3:1 expresses so well what it represents. 'How great is the love the Father has lavished on us, that we should be called children of

God!' (NIV). I love the use of the word 'lavish' here. It always reminds me of a Devon cream tea. My mother-in-law lives in Devon, and so my family and I are often tempted by cream teas. My wife is temperate in all things, including cream teas. She puts a spoonful of jam onto a scone, and then an equal amount of cream. Oh that I was like her! After a modest spoonful of jam I pour or spoon lashings of cream all over it. 'Lavish' describes it perfectly. And 'lavish' is the word which I would choose to describe the overflowing love of God which not only saves us and puts us into the abundant provision of grace described in Romans 5, but actually seeks an organic relationship with us so that we can have God as our Father and be His children.

Familiarity may not always breed contempt, but it usually breeds lack-lustre acceptance, and we have become so used to calling God 'Our Father' that we are guilty often of forgetting what such a title represents. Similarly our kinship with Him can be taken for granted in our spiritual lives, and our hearts can fail to register any reaction when we think of it. But where in human history is there anything like it? – a God of love not just desiring followers and servants, but *children*.

The believers of the Old Testament would have been astonished by such an intimate Father-child relationship. Not for them the close family names: rather the use of distant, awesome, covenantal names such as Jehovah, Elohim, Adonai, El-Shaddai, Jehovah-Jireh. Nowhere in the entire wealth of Jewish devotional literature do we find the name 'father' ever being applied to God. They knew too much of the great gap between God and themselves ever to think of addressing God with such a familiar, everyday family name. The name Jehovah, or more correctly Yahweh, was the most mysterious of all. It was really spelt using the four Hebrew letters Yod-He-

Vav-He which we can write as JHWH. (*) From 300 BC onwards the Jewish Scribes avoided saying it altogether because it was considered too holy, and as a result its pronunciation became unsure. It reminded them of God's awe and uniqueness, and of their lowliness and defilement. God was distant.

The names of God, like the veil in the Temple, represented to the Jews their separation from Him. How God hated that separation and how He longed to be called Father. Even though He had to wait until the coming of His son Jesus Christ before the separation could be healed, God nevertheless made sure that the pages of the Old Testament contained glimpses of that desire which preoccupied Him. While the term 'Father' is only rarely used of God in the Old Testament, and always of His relationship with Israel or with one of His kings, it occurs enough for anyone with eyes to see and ears to hear to understand what was on His heart. Israel should have known.

Exodus 4:22-23 contains the first reference to the Fatherhood of God. God told Moses to reveal to Pharaoh just what God's thoughts were towards His People Israel. Moses was to demand Israel's freedom but more than that was to declare 'Israel is my firstborn son, and I told you, "Let *my son* go, so that he may worship me" ' (NIV). What a revelation! The tragedy is that not only did Pharaoh fail to understand, but the veil of blindness was firmly over Israel's eyes too.

Even when Hosea passionately described God's Father-heart, Israel failed to comprehend it. How beautiful are the fatherly emotions expressed in Hosea 11:1-4 (NIV). 'When Israel was a child, I loved him, and out of Egypt I called my son. But the more I called Israel, the further

(*) This is known as the tetragrammaton.

27

they went from me. They sacrificed to the Baals and they burned incense to images. It was I who taught Ephraim to walk, taking them by the arms; but they did not realise it was I who healed them. I led them with cords of human kindness, with ties of love' (NIV).

Here is a parent in pain; a father lamenting over the idolatrous rebellion of the child He loved and cherished and fondly recalling the days of childhood.

It gives a picture of that important day when God's youngster took his first faltering steps. The crawling had been quickening and more and more he had been pulling himself up on the furniture to a standing position. Suddenly he had rushed into his father's arms and taken his first two or three, never to be forgotten, steps. After that the 'cords of human kindness, with ties of love' applied. These are reins designed to help children still unsteady and weak on their feet to walk – Israel, fondly recalled as a toddler with God's own hand firmly holding him up. A passage of tenderness revealing the loving, caring heart of our God.

But they did not see it or seek to understand. Even David failed to grasp the significance in the promise made by God concerning Solomon 'I will be his Father, and he shall be my son' (2 Samuel 7:14 NIV).

Father had to wait until Jesus appeared on earth. Here at last was the One to satisfy God's heart and bring the Fatherhood of God and His family relationship with believers clearly into view.

Once Jesus had come the emphasis was no more on the separation between God and man, no more on awe and mystery – the emphasis was now on relationship and closeness to God. Jesus constantly addressed God as Father, and used the familiar word 'Abba' which every Jewish family used and still uses. In Aramaic the first two words a child used were 'abba' (daddy) and 'imma' (mummy), and though both words were derived from baby language their use wasn't restricted to children alone 'Abba' was used constantly by adult sons and daughters and it carried with it the warmth and affection we might express by 'dear dad'.

In John's gospel alone Jesus uses the word 'father' about God 100 times! (compared with 15 times in the whole Old Testament). He was the One who would reveal the truth concealed from the foundation of the world.

He used it privately in the agony of Gethsemane. 'Abba, Father . . . everything is possible for you. Take this cup from me. Yet not what I will, but what you will' (Mark 14:36 NIV).

He uses is publicly, 'Jesus looked up and said "Father, I thank you that you have heard me"' and Lazarus was raised from the dead (John 11:41 NIV).

He used it before friends: 'I praise you, Father, Lord of heaven and earth, because you have hidden these things from the wise and learned, and revealed them to little children. Yes, Father, for this was your good pleasure. All things have been committed to me by my Father' (Luke 10:21 and 22 NIV).

He used it before His enemies and was hated for it. 'Jesus said to them, "My Father is always at his work to this very day, and I, too, am working." For this reason the Jews tried all the harder to kill him; not only was He breaking the Sabbath, but he was even calling God His own Father, making Himself equal with God' (John 5:17 and 18 NIV).

It was warm, unceremonious and to the religious people outrageous. Yet it was the most wonderful fact of all creation. God had sent His own Son into the world to save sinners.

If that were the totality of God's plan it would be staggering, but there is more. Not only was God sending

His son, He had a plan to create a whole new family of sons through Him, who would share the exact image and character of Jesus. Jesus was to be 'the firstborn among many brothers' (Romans 8:29 NIV) and was to bring 'many sons to glory' (Hebrews 2:10 NIV).

Can we ever know the excitement and expectation that filled the Father's heart at this point of human history? Let us never underestimate it, nor the wonder of what His Fatherhood means to us.

The highest thing you can give is yourself, and that's what God has given to us by making us His children.

Let us take the example of a sculptor. What is more precious to him, his greatest work of art, or his own child? Obviously his own child.

In the same way God wasn't content to have us as an expression of His creative genius – He wanted us to be His own children. Not for Him a moral resemblance, or a legal agreement between us; not even just a relationship of love, though that would be more than we deserved. He wanted more. Only a unity of life, a family union and likeness, an organic relationship of personality was good enough for Him. He had to have His own life in us. He wanted us eternally united with Him – a permanent link between the Uncreated (God) and the Created (us).

So Jesus had a double-edged message to proclaim: He was God's son but so were the disciples and all who believed in Him. They were to follow His example and address God as Father too. What joy filled Jesus' heart as He proclaimed the Good news. But to the disciples it was such a major departure from all they had known previously, they were probably shocked. Imagine their reaction to the following:-

In Matthew 5 having said that the disciples are 'the salt of the earth' (v13) and 'the light of the world' (v14) Jesus charges them to let their light shine so 'that they may see your good deeds and praise *your Father* in heaven' (v16). Later in the same chapter he tells them to 'Be perfect, therefore, *as your heavenly Father* is perfect' (v48 NIV). In Matthew 6 alone the same truth is repeated no less than twelve times and is constantly reiterated through all four Gospels.

After the resurrection Jesus told Mary to 'go . . . to *my brothers* and tell them, "I am returning to *my Father* and *your Father*, to my God and your God"' (John 20:17 NIV). 'My brother!'

The family of God had come at last and heaven sang with joy. One seed had fallen into the ground and the fields were now white unto harvest.

Isaiah had prophesied of this: 'Yet it was the Lord's will to crush him and cause him to suffer, and though the Lord makes his life a guilt offering, he will *see his offspring* and prolong his days, and the will of the Lord will prosper in his hand' (Isaiah 53:10 NIV).

From these stunning, early revelations, the fact that God is our Father and that we who believe are His children has become well known and well accepted. It no longer surprises us. The New Testament proclaims it as a fundamental truth.

'I will be a Father to you, and you will be my sons and daughters, says the Lord Almighty' (2 Cor. 6:18 NIV).

'For you did not receive a spirit that makes you a slave again to fear, but you received the Spirit of sonship. And by him we cry, "Abba, Father." The Spirit Himself testifies with our spirit that we are God's children' (Romans 8:15 and 16 NIV).

'So you are no longer a slave, but a son' (Gal. 4:7 NIV).

Paul prays to 'the Father' in Ephesians 1:15-23 and Ephesians 3:14 and begins every one of his letters with

'Grace and peace to you from God our Father and from the Lord Jesus Christ' (Romans 1:7 NIV) or a similar phrase.

Jesus is not ashamed to call us brothers and He it was who directed that all prayers should be addressed to the Father.

Notice, however, the balance Jesus tells us to maintain in our prayers: He said 'This is how you should pray: "Our Father in heaven, hallowed be your name"' (Matt. 6:9 NIV). 'Father' spoke of intimacy and closeness, but it was to be followed immediately by 'hallowed be thy name'. 'Hallowed' means to hold in reverence and honour.

It is time that we in the Church remembered this, for in these days of renewal many have been guilty of replacing reverence with an over-familiar, shallow, or even flippant attitude to God. Our closeness to Him should never lead to that – indeed being made His children should cause us to wonder at His love even more and reverence Him in our hearts. We must carefully maintain this balance so that while basking in His love, our honour of Him equals or exceeds that of the Jews of old.

The theme of the Family of God is so important we will develop it further in the next chapter. But before that, it is of deep significance to notice the way in which God had prepared the world for the Saviour's arrival and for the rapid spread of the news He proclaimed.

Galatians 4:4 (NIV) reads 'But when the time had fully come God sent His Son, born of a woman, born under law, to redeem those under law, that we might receive the full rights of sons.'

As a bird prepares the nest for the arrival of its young, so God brought together the threads of history for the birth and life of His own Son. The perfect Man arrived exactly at the time God had sovereignly chosen. The day and hour had been fixed and the Master of History ensured that all was ready.

1. The religious scene was ready

In Exodus 12, where the pattern for the annual Feast of the Passover finds its roots, the Jews were commanded to take a spotless lamb and put it aside for four days (the tenth day to the fourteenth) before slaughtering it. In this God was picturing the time period which would elapse between Adam's sin and the coming of 'the lamb of God', Jesus Christ. When 4,000 years had passed, Jesus arrived on the Earth (a day is as a thousand years). That was the time period which God had sovereignly chosen and Jesus fulfilled it.

The rightness of the time can be seen on many levels. The Old Testament canon, which Ezra had compiled centuries before, was complete, well known and accepted. As it testified of Jesus, it would be the witness to His rightful claim of Messiahship. So Jesus on the road to Emmaus was able 'beginning with Moses and *all* the Prophets' to explain to them 'what was said in all the Scriptures concerning Himself' (Luke 24:27 NIV). He could warn the religious people of His day that they were in error because 'you do not know the Scriptures or the power of God' (Matt. 22:29 NIV). Paul and the early Church could call upon the very Scriptures themselves to justify the Truth they were proclaiming.

Furthermore God had arranged that by the time of Jesus the Jews would be meeting in local synagogues. Synagogues appeared after the exile in Babylon[1] and wherever there was a colony or community of Jews synagogues were erected. This move away from the

1. The Zondervan Pictorial Encyclopaedia. Vol. 5 p554 ff.

centralized worship of the Temple enabled first of all Jesus and later Paul and his companions to speak directly to the Jewish communities themselves. The services were simple, consisting of the reading of the Scriptures, prayer, instruction and a time in which people were asked to speak.

So we find that Jesus went regularly to the synagogues. 'Jesus went throughout Galilee teaching in their synagogues, preaching the good news of the kingdom, and healing every disease and sickness among the people' (Matt. 4:23 NIV).

Paul went straight to the synagogue in Damascus after his conversion. 'Saul spent several days with the disciples in Damascus. At once he began to preach in the synagogues that Jesus is the Son of God' (Acts 9.19 and 20 NIV). Wherever Paul and his partners went the synagogue was their first port of call. God was ensuring that the message would come directly to those for whom it was designed.

Lastly Jesus was given a forerunner, a herald, in the prophetic ministry of John the Baptist. No king could ever be legitimately recognized unless he was supported by the word of a Prophet, and John the Baptist, born six months earlier than Jesus, was the one chosen to testify of Him. To deny the right to the throne of one proclaimed by a recognized Prophet was a very serious matter.

Jesus was able to call upon this testimony when the chief priests questioned His right to speak as He did. Jesus replied 'I will also ask you one question. If you answer me, I will tell you by what authority I am doing these things. John's baptism – where did it come from? Was it from heaven, or from men?' They discussed it among themselves and said, 'If we say, "From heaven," he will ask, "Then why didn't you believe him?" But if we say, "from men" – we are afraid of the people, for they all hold that John was a prophet.'

So they answered Jesus, 'We don't know.'

Then he said, 'Neither will I tell you by what authority I am doing these things' (Matt. 21:24-27 NIV).

The timing was perfect.

2. The cultural scene was ready

Anyone who has ever tried to communicate to a group of people through an interpreter will tell you how frustrating it is! Not only is the rate of progress slowed down but the momentum is lost. Speaking through only one interpreter is bad enough, but I have often had to speak to a 'mixed multitude' where two or more interpreters have been necessary. The difficulty is not just that of feeling frustrated at the difficulty of communication, but actually keeping your mind on the subject. You might begin by saying 'Jesus said', but by the time the interpreters have spoken and it is your turn again, you often can't remember what it was that Jesus had said!

The confusion of language at the Tower of Babel was designed to slow down the spread of apostasy, but it could also act as a barrier to spreading the Gospel. God overcame this through Alexander the Great. At the time of Alexander the Greek peninsula was occupied by several distinct groups of Greeks who all spoke different Greek dialects. Alexander knew that if Greece was to become great and defend herself successfully against her enemies it was no use having linguistic barriers to overcome. He knew they had to have a common Greek language. Under his rule common or Koine Greek became accepted by all the Greeks and he was able to galvanize them into a united military machine. This brilliant General conquered the then known world, and when he died at the age of thirty-three in Babylon his Empire stretched from Greece and North Africa to India and the borders of China.

35

Everywhere he went he insisted that Greek should be taught and spoken, and it became the lingua franca of every country.

When Jesus came to the Earth this common Greek was known in all the Mediterranean World. The Jews even had the Old Testament written in it. So it was that the preaching of the Apostles and early Church spread like wildfire. A common language enabled all to hear and understand the Good News.

How much more slowly would the message have been spread without God's perfect planning and timing.

3. The Political Scene Was Ready

The Ancient World was a rough tough place. Living in a walled city was hazardous enough without taking on the added danger of travelling to preach.

Yet God chose the very time when the might of Rome stretched from France and the German borders to Egypt. The Roman armies had brought peace and stability all around the Mediterranean lands, and with them had come excellent roads and communications. It was boasted that you could travel from one end of the Mediterranean to the other without needing a weapon.

In fact the conditions were the best the world had ever seen, and down these Roman roads poured Christians of every description telling the nations that Jesus was risen from the dead, and encouraging one another in fellowship.

No other time in history could have been more perfect and it stands as a testimony to the Lord of history that He and He alone could bring together so many historical events at the very time His Son was born.

God, like any Father, would ensure that the news of the arrival of His family would be quickly and fully broadcast.

3

The Family of God

Jesus said 'I tell you the truth, unless a man is born again, he cannot see the kingdom of God' (John 3:3 NIV). 'Born again? Born again?' The old man stroked his beard, his furrowed brow showing total incomprehension. He was *the* teacher in Israel, Gamaliel's successor, more wise and knowledgeable than all; how was it that he had never heard of such a concept before?

Being born again could only mean one thing: that one had a new beginning. Was Jesus really saying that people who had been born into this world, who had inherited characteristics and weaknesses from their parents, and who had then been hardened and moulded by the experiences of life could start again? It could not be.

'"How can a man be born when he is old?" Nicodemus asked. "Surely he cannot enter a second time into his mother's womb to be born again!"' (John 3:4 NIV). Jesus' response to this teacher of the Jews was the only one He could give. Why did Nicodemus find this so difficult? Had not Israel, the nation Nicodemus was proud to belong to, had a double birth? Descended from Abraham, Israel had been born again into nationhood at the Exodus when God had sent the wind to open a channel through the Red Sea. Surely Nicodemus knew that. 'Jesus answered, "I tell you the truth, unless a man is born of water and the Spirit (lit. wind[1]), he cannot enter the kingdom of God' (John 3:5 NIV).

We must not try to Christianize this – Jesus was speaking to a Jew, not a Christian, and the 'water and the wind' would mean nothing else but the Exodus to him. There had been no Promised Land for Israel in Egypt, even though they were God's people: only after a miraculous move of God and a journey through the opened waters of the Red Sea could they come into it. 'Flesh gives birth to flesh, but the Spirit gives birth to spirit' (John 3:6 NIV), and it was the Spirit of God which had given birth to the nation of Israel.

Thus it was that Nicodemus became convinced of the most important fact of human existence; that even though we have natural families from whom we have inherited natural characteristics, God is offering all of us a new birth which will make us part of a spiritual family, sons in the family of God Himself.

All who believe have been born twice in this way, and all Christians therefore belong to both a natural and a spiritual family.

As a teenager I had a deep yearning to discover my roots and had tried to glean from my uncles and aunts details of my long dead relatives. It wasn't just a passing interest either, it was a passionate pursuit. Were the two Wadham sisters who had dispossessed my grandmother because she had run off and married a wheelwright really still alive? Who was George or 'Lifey' Ryall, and why had I and my father been given his name as one of our Christian names? Had my great-grandmother really been married four times? I had to know.

I'm sure that if God had not intervened my passion would have blossomed into the fanaticism of my recently

1. Spirit and wind are the same Greek word – Pneuma.

dead second cousin Georgina. An American, she had spent many years trying to trace the ancestry of my grandmother whose maiden name was Martha Annie Ryall. Georgina had been convinced that the surname 'Ryall' was in its original form 'Royal' and was, therefore, an echo of days of former glory. She dreamed of the day when she could write to the Queen of England as 'Dear Cousin Elizabeth'.

After my conversion I realized that my passion had not been based on such proud foundations, and had been simply the attempt of one insignificant, transient speck of dust to find some sense of purpose and meaning. It was my attempt to get a form of eternal life.

Once I had the real thing, however, my natural family roots faded in significance. My spiritual lineage was now of paramount importance to me, and it was so much more simple too. God is a Father only and has no grand-children, so grandparents and great-grandparents don't figure. God is the Father and all who believe are the first generation. But this only occurs with a new or second birth. The idea that all belong to God's family and that there is therefore a Universal Brotherhood of Man is not found in the Bible. As Harold Macmillan said, 'You can't have the Universal Brotherhood of Man without first having the Universal Fatherhood of God.'

Without the second birth – 'the Spirit giving birth to spirit' (John 3:6 NIV) – it is impossible to be a member of God's family. It is not automatic. Jesus was very clear on this point, especially to the religious Jews who were all banking on the fact that they were physically descended from Abraham. He said 'If God were your Father, you would love me, for I came from God and now am here . . . . You belong to your father, the devil . . . . He who belongs to God hears what God says. The reason you do not hear is that you do not belong to God' (John 8:42–44 and 47 NIV).

To all of us Jesus says 'Whoever believes in the Son has

eternal life, but whoever rejects the Son will not see life, for God's wrath remains on him' (John 3:36 NIV).

God desires all men to be His children and has made it possible through the sacrifice of His Son Jesus. The tragedy is that so few will respond to His desire and actually believe and put their trust in His Son. God 'wants all men to be saved and to come to a knowledge of the truth' (1 Tim. 2:4 NIV) but 'men loved darkness rather than light' (John 3:19). John 1 sums up the whole matter: He 'was in the world, and though the world was made through Him, the world did not recognize Him. He came to that which was His own, but His own did not receive Him. Yet to all who received him, to those who believed in His name, He gave the right to become children of God – children born not of natural descent, nor of human decision or a husband's will, but born of God' (John 1: 10-13 NIV).

We who have believed have been born twice and so we belong to both a physical and a spiritual family. As our relationship with God the Father and the Lord Jesus deepens so inevitably will our love for our spiritual family. Obviously we still have a love for and a responsibility to our natural families, but often our love for our spiritual brothers and sisters exceeds that of any natural connection.[1] Our unbelieving natural families obviously find this hard to understand, but they do not appreciate how real the spiritual family is. Occasionally there is an actual conflict between our loyalty to our heavenly Father and our loyalty to them and the difficult guidance of Jesus is that *in such circumstances* our spiritual loyalty must come first.

1. This is not meant in any way to contravene the obvious injunction given to us that we must fulfil our responsibilities as parents to our children, wives or husbands whether they be believers or not. Christian husbands and wives should be an extra blessing to their unconverted spouses. Similarly Christian children must show their unbelieving parents greater honour and love and obey them as unto the Lord.

'If anyone comes to me and does not hate his father and mother, his wife and children, his brothers and sisters – yes, even his own life – he cannot be my disciple. And anyone who does not carry his cross and follow me cannot be my disciple' (Luke 14:26 and 27 NIV). Usually such a division does not have to occur, but we must search our hearts about this.

For example a friend of mine who, like me, was converted at University was told to choose. His father said 'It's either Jesus or me! If it's Jesus, you won't be allowed back in the house.' My friend left sorrowfully, unable to compromise his stand for Jesus. Though his father has not been saved to date, he has relented and allowed his son back. I am certain that my friend's stand has spoken volumes to him.

Frequently the natural family order is mixed up by the new birth. When you are born-again your believing grandfather becomes your brother; your Christian mother is at the same time your sister. I was instrumental in leading my father to Christ and not only, therefore, were we brothers, but I was the elder brother too. Such are the interesting possibilities inherent in the spiritual birth.

The older a Christian is, the more clearly the spiritual family and its responsibilities come into focus. Nowhere is this more clearly seen that in the developing life of Jesus. After all He combined the spiritual and the natural, the heavenly and the earthly, right from His birth. His mother was human, His Father was God Himself. The angel reassured Joseph about this just after Joseph had heard of Mary's pregnancy. The angel said 'Joseph son of David, do not be afraid to take Mary home as your wife, because what is conceived in her is from the Holy Spirit' (Matt. 1:20 NIV). Today many laugh at the idea of the virgin birth, but they are guilty of the serious error of limiting God's activity. To dare to say that God cannot or will not do something, is to box him in and reduce Him to human proportions. Those who do this are also guilty of glorifying humanity and making all Christianity man-centred instead of God-centred. The rank unbelief and apostasy at the root of such doubt is horrifying.

The testimony of the Bible is that Jesus had God Himself as His Father. Matthew's Gospel states this as a fact and then confirms it in a fascinating way. In the first chapter Matthew sums up the genealogy of Christ by saying 'Thus there were fourteen generations in all from Abraham to David, fourteen from David to the exile in Babylon, and fourteen from the exile to the Christ' (Matt. 1:17 NIV). A careful examination of the listed names, however, reveals that whereas the first two have fourteen names each, the third and last list has only 13! Joseph, 'the husband of Mary, of whom was born Jesus, who is called Christ' is the 12th. Jesus, the last. Who is missing? Why the very father of Jesus, God Himself. The following list shows this clearly:-

1. Abraham	1. Solomon	1. Shealtiel
2. Isaac	2. Rehoboam	2. Zerubbabel
3. Jacob	3. Abijah	3. Abuid
4. Judah	4. Asa	4. Eliakim
5. Perez	5. Jehoshaphat	5. Azor
6. Hezron	6. Joram	6. Zadok
7. Ram	7. Uzziah	7. Akim
8. Amminadab	8. Jotham	8. Eliud
9. Nashon	9. Ahaz	9. Eleazar
10. Salmon	10. Hezekiah	10. Mattham
11. Boaz	11. Manasseh	11. Jacob
12. Obed	12. Aman	12. Joseph
13. Jesse	13. Josiah	13. GOD the FATHER
14. David	14. Jeconiah	14. Jesus

Joseph was faithful to God in that he married Mary, 'but he had no union with her until she gave birth to a son. And he gave him the name Jesus' (Matt. 1:25 NIV).

Once Jesus was born, Mary and Joseph went on to have at least seven of their own children. These are listed for us in Matthew 13:55 and 56. 'Isn't this the carpenter's son?' Isn't his mother's name Mary, and aren't his brothers James, Joseph, Simon and Judas? Aren't all his sisters with us?' He had four brothers and (as the word 'all' shows us) at least three sisters.

Actually these were half brothers and sisters of Jesus, for whereas they all had Mary as their mother, they had a different father. Jesus' father was God Himself; their father was Joseph.

The people looking on, seeing only the natural family of Jesus and not discerning his heavenly roots, were therefore justifiably amazed with Jesus' learning and understanding. No wonder they looked at one another and said 'Where then did this man get all these things?' (Matt. 13:56 NIV). It was from His Father in heaven, not His natural descent.

As Jesus' life unfolds, this division between Jesus' natural relatives and His spiritual family becomes more and more clear. We see it first in His childhood, then in His Ministry and finally, gloriously, at His death.

Jesus' Childhood

The Bible maintains an almost total silence about the life of Jesus before His Ministry began. The one exception to this is the significant episode which occurred when Jesus was a boy of twelve. It shines out of the veil of silence because of the important revelations it contains about Jesus' spiritual family.

Luke 2:41-50 gives the details.

'Every year his parents went to Jerusalem for the Feast of the Passover. When he was twelve years old, they went up to the Feast according to the custom. After the Feast was over, while his parents were returning home, the boy Jesus stayed behind in Jerusalem but they were unaware of it. Thinking he was in their company, they travelled on for a day. Then they began looking for him among their relatives and friends. When they did not find him, they went back to Jerusalem to look for him. After three days they found him in the temple courts, sitting among the teachers, listening to them and asking them questions. Everyone who heard him was amazed at his understanding and his answers. When his parents saw him, they were astonished. His mother said to him, 'Son, why have you treated us like this? Your father and I have been anxiously searching for you.' 'Why were you searching for me?' he asked. 'Didn't you know I had to be in my Father's house?' But they did not understand what he was saying to them' (NIV).

It might seem unthinkable to most parents that Jesus could have been missing and unnoticed for one whole day's journey. The explanation is, however, very simple. Whole families travelled together and it was customary for the women to travel in a group ahead of the men. Whereas the young children accompanied the women, the older children were permitted to travel in either group. As a result it would have been very simple for Mary to think Jesus was with Joseph, and for Joseph to think he was with Mary.

When the mistake had been discovered, the family turned back to Jerusalem, and began to search for him. We are not told whether Joseph or Mary had any relatives living in Jerusalem, but if they had, their first reaction would have been to go to the relatives' houses. A lost boy would naturally head for a home he knew. If that drew a blank, the market places and play areas would be next on the list.

After three days' searching they finally went to the Temple, and there to their amazement they found Jesus. Relaxed and enjoying Himself, He was deep in discussion with the teachers and learned men.

His parents were astonished and understandably taken aback; but Jesus said 'Why were you searching for me? Didn't you know I had to be in my Father's house?' (v49).

Jesus' reply has been misunderstood. It isn't the retort of a rebellious child, nor that of a precocious young man; it was the reply of a son who had gone to His Father's house to wait for His family. God was His Father and what more obvious place could He have sought? The Temple was home to Him.

Twelve years had elapsed since His birth, and both Mary and Joseph had needed the reminder that Jesus belonged to another family as well as theirs. Of course neither of them really understood, but they knew enough to know this was significant. The account continues by saying that Mary 'treasured all these things in her heart' (Luke 2:51 NIV).

Luke's account ends beautifully. 'And Jesus grew in wisdom and stature and in favour with God and men' (v52 NIV).

What better testimonial could a boy have than that? The division between the natural and spiritual family had begun.

Jesus Ministry

The next revelation of this division occurred at a teaching session at least eighteen years later. The scene was a crowded house.

I love the story very much because the first public

Bible Study I attended was in a similar place. It occurred in 1968 when I was in Reading. A minister had been invited to come and teach the Word and news of the visit was spread far and wide. I had been taught always to arrive at a place on time, or if that were not possible to be late rather than early. 'Never be early if you can avoid it' was the rule which I had learned as a child. I hadn't realized that the rules which applied if you were going out to dinner at someone's house (to avoid the embarrassment of finding the host and hostess still busy in the kitchen and not yet changed ready to receive their guests) didn't apply to Christian meetings. So I had walked around the block three or four times to ensure that I wouldn't be early.

Praise was already in full swing as I walked up the path, and I will never forget the sight which met my gaze when I entered the house. Every available space, every nook and cranny, was occupied.

The dividing partition between the rooms had been removed but still there was not enough room. The windowsills were occupied, some people were sitting under the keyboard of the piano and the cushions on the fireplace were obscured by bodies. I was told that the kitchen was full too, and that the only place for me was halfway up the stairs. The speaker was going to stand in the doorway and so it was not going to be too bad a position.

I pitied the few late stragglers who came in – they had obviously mis-timed their polite timewasting! – the place had breathing room only.

How vividly this comes to my mind when I read Matthew 12: 46-50. In that house-meeting 2000 years ago Jesus was the speaker, and so large was the crowd that when His mother, Mary, and His half-brothers James, Joseph, Simon and Judas arrived wanting to speak with

Him, they could not get within shouting distance.

You can imagine the message being passed along from person to person, and finally one person having to interrupt the teaching session to tell Jesus that His family had arrived and needed to speak to Him.

Today the interrupting telephone can be quietly answered and the promise made to call back afterwards, but a visit from one's relatives would cause any speaker to stop and go and see what urgent matter had brought them.

Jesus, however, uses this opportunity to reveal just how different are the natural and spiritual families. 'Someone told him, "Your mother and brothers are standing outside wanting to speak to you"' (Matt. 12:47 NIV). A simple, straightforward statement, and yet what a response it evoked. Before an astonished crowd Jesus asked 'Who is my mother, and who are my brothers?' (v48 NIV). He then pointed to the disciples and said 'Here are my mother and my brothers' (v49 NIV)!!

To the natural mind it was just a crazy, nonsensical statement, but in the revelation of the new birth it was nothing but plain fact. The disciples were part of His spiritual family (a family in which were no male or female divisions), and hence were His mother and brothers. It was truth on a different plane with power to liberate whoever received it from the limitations of their natural inheritance.

Then He gave one sentence of explanation: 'For whoever does the will of my Father in heaven is my brother and sister and mother' (v50 NIV). What is the will of the Father? It is defined for us in John 6:28 (NIV) 'The work of God is this: to believe in the one he has sent'. All who believe become children of God, and as members of God's family are related to one another. John completes the theme in his first epistle – adding that we must also love one another.

The new birth creates the family; the love makes it a coherent recognizable reality.

The last glimpse which Jesus gave us of the reality of the spiritual family clearly demonstrates the necessity for this love.

Jesus' Death

Jesus uttered seven statements while hanging on the cross. The writer Arthur W. Pink[1] describes them as follows:-

1. *The Word of Forgiveness.*

'Then said Jesus, "Father, forgive them; for they know not what they do"' (Luke 23:34).

2. *The Word of Salvation.*

'Then he said, "Jesus, remember me when you come into your kingdom." Jesus answered him, "I tell you the truth, today you will be with me in paradise"' (Luke 23: 42 and 43 NIV).

3. *The Word of Affection.*

'Near the cross of Jesus stood his mother, his mother's sister, Mary the wife of Clopas, and Mary of Magdala. When Jesus saw his mother there, and the disciple whom he loved standing nearby, he said to his mother, "Dear woman, here is your son"' (John 19:25 and 26 NIV).

4. *The Word of Anguish.*

'About the ninth hour Jesus cried out in a loud voice, "Eloi, Eloi, Lama sabachthani?" – which means, "My God, my God, why have you forsaken me?"' (Matt. 27:46 NIV).

1. Arthur W. Pink. 'The Seven Sayings of Jesus on the Cross'. Baker Book House.

5. *The Word of Suffering.*

'Later, knowing that all was now completed, and so that the Scripture would be fulfilled, Jesus said, "I am thirsty."' (John 19:28 NIV).

6. *The Word of Victory.*

'When he had received the drink, Jesus said, "It is finished." With that, he bowed his head and gave up his spirit' (John 19:30 NIV).

7. *The Word of Contentment.*

'Jesus called out with a loud voice, "Father, into your hands I commit my spirit." When he had said this, he breathed his last' (Luke 23:46 NIV).

Almost every part of our salvation is covered by these seven sayings.

But it is the 'Word of Affection' which engages our attention here. Jesus looked with compassion on His widowed mother, but rather than entrust her to her seven natural children (at least two of whom, James and Judas, would be converted later). 'He turned to them and said "Dear woman, here is your son," and to the disciple, "Here is your mother"' (John 19:26 and 27 NIV). John adds 'From that time on, this disciple took her into his home' (v 27). She lived with John until she died.

We need to look around us in our churches and fellowships and acknowledge one another with the thought 'my mother, my son, my daughter, my brother, my sister.'

What a glorious thing: God's family lives on this fallen Earth and shows to the whole world that love, unity and happiness is possible through the new birth.

After our wedding in 1978 one of my Socialist uncles, a Welsh ex-miner and councillor announced to the left-wing Socialist convention in Aberystwyth that he had seen with his own eyes what he had spent his life trying to achieve – a loving, selfless, coherent group of people. 'The Christians have got it' he said.

But all of this comes only through the new birth. The story is often told of the Christian preacher at Hyde Park Corner who was assailed by a communist (they imagine communism to be so practical!) with the jibe 'Communism can put a new coat on this man.' Unhesitatingly, the preacher replied 'Ah yes, but Christianity can put a new man in this coat.' The truth is wonderful in its simplicity and in its power. No-one who is born into the family of God can ever be the same again.

4

Like Father, Like Son

The Times carried a report recently which said that 60% of all children stop studying history at the age of 14. As a firm believer that a knowledge of history is essential to understand the present world and that 'those who ignore the lessons of history are prone to relive them', I shook my head in despair. When I read it to my wife she was appalled, but then recalled that she too had given up formal history early. It then dawned on me that because at the school I went to we had to make a choice between geography and history at the beginning of the fourth year, I too had done the same!

If I had known then what I know now, my choice of 'O' levels would have been very different indeed. I would definitely have studied biology and concentrated on the laws of genetics, and would not have allowed my overwhelming love of chemistry to eclipse it as it did. But the fact is that no-one can force an old head onto young shoulders.

As a convinced Creationist I know that the 'kind begets kind' law stated ten times in Genesis 1 is correct and that whereas some variation, adjustment and adaptation may occur within each kind, there is never a leaping over the 'kind' boundaries. As I wrote in my book *In the Beginning*[1]:

1. *In the Beginning* Roger Price. Reprinted by New Wine Press.

'We have several categories in the initial creation. The restriction was that they could only reproduce within the confines of their own group, and that no group could produce offspring of another group although development within the kinds could occur.'

'So the cat family is one kind – it has many different types of cat within it but all the forms of cats can be traced back to the originally created cats. Cats will never produce non-cats – the kind is fixed. Variation and adaptation can occur within the kind but will never cross the 'kind' boundaries. So dogs didn't originate from the cat kind, dogs came from the dog kind. There are at present over 200 varieties of dog all capable of interbreeding but they are all dogs and always will be.'

The rule is fixed. Darwin himself researched the finches of the Galapagos Islands and chronicled many variations and changes, but all of them were definitely finches.

When Jesus said 'Flesh gives birth to flesh, but the Spirit gives birth to spirit', He was affirming that the same absolute rule applies in our salvation. No matter what the flesh tries to produce, no matter how much religious activity it indulges in, it can only produce fleshly, natural results. To become a spiritual being, to belong to the family of God, requires a new birth and the formation of a new 'kind'.

This is the teaching of John 1:12-13. 'To all who received him, to those who believed in his name, he gave the right to become children of God – children born not of natural descent, nor of human decision or a husband's will, but born of God' (NIV). The new birth described here is 'not of natural descent'. The Jews thought they were saved because they had the genes of Abraham in them. That's not good enough, for flesh can only produce flesh; heredity cannot get you across the 'kind' boundary.

Neither can all the decision, determination and effort in the world. Nor can another human being's efforts. The only thing that can make us children of God is that we are 'born of God'. Once God is our Father then we belong to a new category of creation and are truly heavenly people.

2 Corinthians 5:17 says it clearly: 'Therefore, if anyone is in Christ, he is a new creation' (NIV). We could say 'a new creature', or 'a new kind' and this verse confirms that the 'kind begets kind' principle applies in the new birth. Indeed 1 John 3:9 uses the language of Genesis when it says of every believer that 'God's seed remains in him' (NIV). Peter too confirms it 'For you have been born again, not of perishable seed, but of imperishable, through the living and enduring word of God' (1 Peter 1:23 NIV).

So we can trace our roots straight back to God and we should be able to see His characteristics in us. This certainly applies in the physical or natural realm – we are only too aware of the features and traits of character we have inherited naturally – so why should we think that it doesn't in the spiritual realm. Let us examine natural inheritance to see the principle clearly.

A child's parents are the source of the characteristics he exhibits. Just how true this is came home to me forcibly when watching a group of children, my own included, running and jumping in a playing field. Someone standing next to me said 'Roger, David runs just like you!' It had been many years since someone had commented on the fact that I had a distinctive running style, and at that time I just hadn't known what they meant. As I looked at my son, however, I could see it. What is interesting is that, as far as I know, he hadn't copied my style of running and hadn't learned it from me. He had inherited it!

When you deliberately watch out for these things it is fascinating to see the similarities and variations. My daughter Karen is always pretending she is a doctor or nurse and tending the wounded soldiers; she loves gardening, and plants, and has a lovely little turned up nose. We don't have to look far to see where she got this. She also loves books and music and is very determined, like someone else we know!

David loves books, maps and mathematics like me, but also has a flair for art like my wife. He is full of bravado one minute and timidity the next. Like me he always finds reserves of energy when, although he is really tired out, friends or visitors suddenly arrive. Watch out afterwards, though!

Both of them are little actors. From the age of 9 I was writing plays and with a group of friends performing them in our back garden. The entrance fee was one penny and we gave refreshments free. Any profit was spent on sets or make-up. How remarkable therefore that when visiting a Christian friend, both my children suddenly pulled open some curtains with a pretend fanfare and proceeded to put on a performance!

My wife and I take full responsibility for it all. There are, however, definite characteristics which, while passed on by us, are from their grandparents. Ros and I have thick wavy hair and yet both our youngsters have fine, totally straight hair. It would seem that people with curly or wavy hair yearn for straight hair and vice versa but, for myself, it is only now that I realize what problems are associated with straight hair. Where did they both get it from? We need look no further than my mother – indeed one of my sisters has exactly the same type of hair. Both children are very practical as were both grandfathers. I could go on and on and I am sure all parents could do the same.

Teachers, too, regularly meet the unalterable laws of inheritance. How often have they understood the problems of a boy or girl pupil the moment they meet their parents! About to analyse 'little Johnny's personality block', I had on many occasions to change what I was going to say as I saw the older version sitting before me.

This is actually the strength of a family, for if parents can recognize their own personalities and problems in their children, they often know how best to deal with them from their own experience.

How I praise God for a wise father who, though a non-Christian at the time, recognized in me his own temper, rebellion and stubbornness. When he also saw that it was mixed with George (or Lifey) Ryall's vivid personality, he realized that it was potentially a cocktail for disaster. He knew that his weaknesses had been controlled by strict discipline and so he knew full well that it was what I needed too. My bottom was often sore – I went to a school that used the cane liberally too. Correct discipline isn't designed to break a child's spirit but basically to teach him how to control himself. It certainly did me a world of good.

The Bible speaks about the discipline of children and supports the use of corporal punishment.

'He who spares the rod hates his son, but he who loves him is careful to discipline him' (Proverbs 13:24 NIV).

'Folly is bound up in the heart of a child, but the rod of discipline will drive it far from him' (Proverbs 22:15 NIV).

There is no way that the Bible believing Christian can ignore these verses – the rod cannot be explained away as purely as a measuring rod.

It is essential that a balance is maintained, for although the Bible supports corporal punishment, it nowhere supports child-beating. What is interesting to note is that nowhere in the Bible is exact instruction given on this.

The Law of God doesn't say that every child who lies must be given one stroke, every one who steals two strokes and so on. The decision is in the hands of the parent. The wise parent knows and understands his child, and will administer punishment accordingly. I needed a firm, strict upbringing and thankfully received it. A different child must have been damaged or become nervous with the same treatment. The application of correct discipline is part of the art of parenthood. Aristotle said 'To treat unequals equally is the greatest form of inequality.' I do not often support Greek philosophers, but I have to agree with him on this.

Any discipline which does not come from a parent's desire to train his or her child and teach that child self-restraint is wrong. Vengeance, selfishness, impatience and any similar motive become damaging. 'Train a child in the way he should go' (Proverbs 22:6 NIV) is the golden rule behind it all. It is positive and creative, not negative and destructive. We must not be afraid to administer discipline as many suggest today. God demands that parents apply discipline.

Eli was severely reprimanded and judged, together with his whole family, because 'his sons made themselves contemptible, and he failed to restrain them' (1 Sam. 3:13 NIV). The Bible is the highest authority and we neglect it at our peril[1]. But it must be rightly applied. Who better to apply it than parents, who not only love and understand their child but probably have similar traits and characteristics themselves?

There are very definite spiritual parallels we can draw

1. The posturing of many humanists today is horrifying. While all of us recognize a breakdown in discipline and personal restraint, these misguided do-gooders are constantly advocating less and less restraint and more and more self-expression. The blind leading the blind can only end with both in the ditch.

56

from this, for if we have inherited so much from our natural parents through our first birth, how much more have we inherited from our Father in heaven? Our spiritual birth is more powerful and dynamic than our natural birth and, if allowed, can dominate and overcome any natural inheritance.

Jeremiah asked 'Can the Ethiopian change his skin or the leopard its spots?' (Jer. 13:23 NIV). In the natural realm the answer is 'No', because a 'kind' cannot change into another 'kind', but with the new birth there is another family likeness in us which is just as real and just as distinct and which can change our whole lives. 'But if Christ is in you, your body is dead because of sin, yet your spirit is alive because of righteousness. And if the Spirit of him who raised Jesus from the dead is living in you, he who raised Christ from the dead will also give life to your mortal bodies through his Spirit, who lives in you' (Romans 8:10 and 11 NIV).

It is a real inheritance from God Himself. Be careful not to miss what this means. Peter says 'His divine power has given us everything we need for life and godliness through our knowledge of him who called us by his own glory and goodness. Through these he has given us his very great and precious promises, so that through them *you may participate in the divine nature* and escape the corruption in the world caused by evil desires' (2 Peter 1:3 and 4 NIV).

As God is our Father then of course we have within us His Divine nature, and if we allow it to, it will grow, develop and eventually dominate our whole being. If my children are in so many ways 'chips off the old block', how much more powerfully must the character of God come out in us His children. Again Jesus emphasises the effect that the new birth has. As He continued explaining the new birth to Nicodemus Jesus underlined the dynamic power associated with it. Having affirmed the 'kind begets kind' principle by saying 'flesh gives birth to flesh, but the Spirit gives birth to spirit,' He said 'you should not be surprised at my saying, "You must be born again. The wind blows wherever it pleases. You hear its sound, but you cannot tell where it comes from or where it is going. So it is with everyone born of the Spirit"' (John 3:6-8 NIV). Perhaps as He spoke the wind was whistling around the place where they were, and the leaves of the trees were rustling.

So Jesus drew a parallel between the wind and the effects of the spiritual birth. First of all both the wind and the spirit are invisible, but they have very real effects, some immediate, some taking a little longer. Whereas many problems in my life took some time to be dealt with and be removed, my temper left immediately. My family will testify to the fact that I was an angry young man and liable to 'fly off the handle' frequently at the least provocation. It was a sudden, violent eruption which occurred without warning. A quiet discussion would often end with my storming off or with my fist heading for someone's mouth. The Spirit of God removed my uncontrollable temper instantly.

One woman I know stopped smoking straight away; another who had dabbled in the forbidden occultic practice of reading Tarot cards and who had a hardened, mask-like face looked up after giving her life to Jesus and her face was radiant and shining. There are so many examples.

As we grow in our Christian lives the alteration becomes more widespread and noticeable – 'Now the Lord is the Spirit, and where the Spirit of the Lord is, there is freedom. And we, who with unveiled faces all reflect the Lord's glory, are being transformed into his likeness with ever-increasing glory, which comes from the

Lord, who is the Spirit' (2 Cor. 3:17-18 NIV).

Just as a force 10^1 wind can blow over trees, overturn boats, rip off roofs and demolish walls, even though invisible, so the Spirit of God is 'divine power to demolish strongholds' (2 Cor. 10:4 NIV). Once the Spirit of God blows into a person's life they will never be the same again.

Following on from this, however, is the lesson of freedom. The wind represented to the ancient world total, unbounded freedom. No one could control it, or direct it or determine its effects. As Jesus said 'The wind blows wherever it pleases' (John 3:8 NIV).

Today we have sophisticated meteorological satellites and weather stations, yet so complex are the high and low pressure systems and thermal exchange mechanisms which control the pattern and force of our winds that it is still impossible to forecast what a weather system will do with complete accuracy. Weather men are criticized for their errors in forecasting and always will be. 'You hear its sound, but you cannot tell where it comes from or where it is going' (John 3:8 NIV).

Who can control the wind? Even in these days of triple glazing, cavity-wall insulation, loft insulation, even with feathers falling unmolested down the window panes, one's feet can gradually turn to ice as the little draught blows freely around from we know not where. The wind is still completely free.

'So it is with everyone born of the Spirit' (John 3:8 NIV). Here is the climax of his argument. Everyone born from above comes into the realm of total freedom; 'the glorious freedom of the children of God' (Romans 8:21 NIV).

What a contrast between the old life and the new! One a life of guilt, bondage, unhappiness, fruitless toil, and

1. The Beaufort wind scale.

desperation; the other a life of forgiveness, liberty, unspeakable joy, reward in heaven and contentment. No wonder Jesus used the analogy of Israel before and after the Exodus as His example with Nicodemus. Before the Exodus Israel was under Pharoah's heel, beaten, whipped and oppressed; but afterwards they were a free and glorious nation. What a testimony this is to a world which has no such choice; a world enslaved to sin.

The fallen nature inherited from our natural birth and hitherto so dominant in our lives can now gradually fade and its grip be loosened by the new nature, which is after all the very character of God Himself. All we have to do is set our mind on what God has done in us and put off the old. Formerly we had no choice; now we have.

'Therefore, brothers, we have an obligation – but it is not to the sinful nature, to live according to it. For if you live according to the sinful nature, you will die; but if by the Spirit you put to death the misdeeds of the body, you will live' (Romans 8:12-13 NIV).

'You were taught, with regard to your former way of life, to put off your old self, which is being corrupted by its deceitful desires; to be made new in the attitude of your minds; and to put on the new self, created to be like God in true righteousness and holiness' (Eph. 4: 22-24 NIV).

God does not patch up and revamp the old, He makes a brand new creation, 'the new man . . . after the image of him that created him' (Col. 3:10 NIV).

As Jesus showed the character of the Father, so the new birth has produced the same in us. When Philip asked Jesus if he could see the Father, Jesus replied 'Anyone who has seen me has seen the Father' (John 14:9 NIV). That is the exact extent of the heredity. God was His Father and so you could see the Father in Him. God is also our Father and, therefore, like our brother Jesus, Father is in us.

This is the constant message of the New Testament. At the point of salvation we became God's children and new life was imparted to us. That new life is the very life of God Himself and as we allow it to take full control we are changed into the likeness of Jesus. He was born from the seed of God and so are we. That means that potentially all that was seen in Jesus can be seen in us too. 'As He is, so are we in this world' (1 John 4:17 NIV).

Indeed one of the most important purposes of our lives is that Jesus might be seen in us. Paul actually describes his salvation in these terms. 'But when God, who set me apart from birth and called me by his grace, was pleased *to reveal* his Son in me so that I might preach him among the Gentiles, I did not consult any man . . . . ' (Gal. 1:15 NIV). Indeed we are 'predestined to be conformed to the likeness of his Son, that he might be the firstborn among many brothers' (Romans 8:29 NIV). The seed will come to full fruit.

We are from the same genetic stock as our Saviour, we share the same Father, and therefore the results should be the same. The fruit of the Spirit[1], described so graphically in Galatians 5:22-23 is nothing other than the very character of Jesus. When, therefore, Paul tells us to be 'imitators of God' (Eph. 5:1 NIV) he is not telling us to do something we cannot do, but something which is gloriously possible.

Many of the New Testament statements about what we can do and are expected to do are based on the reality of the 'like father-like son' principle we have outlined. As we have seen previously, Jesus' explanation for the fact that the religious Jews failed to recognize Him and understand what He was saying, was that they would not

1. For a fuller discussion of the fruit of the Spirit, see my book *Possessing the Land*. New Wine Press/Marshalls.

because they were not children of God. God was not their Father. John declares that this still applies: 'We are from God, and whoever knows God listens to us; but whoever is not from God does not listen to us. This is how we recognize the Spirit of truth and the spirit of falsehood' (1 John 4:6 NIV).

You have to be a member of God's family in order to recognize Jesus and any other family members. But once in the family, the family likeness will show up and soon we will be acting and responding in the manner of Jesus Himself.

We quoted earlier 1 Peter 1:23 which stated that we were born again of incorruptible seed. It is vital that we note the context carefully, for this statement about imperishable seed follows a statement about our love for one another. 'As obedient children, do not conform to the evil desires you had when you lived in ignorance. But just as he who called you is holy, so be holy in all you do' (1 Peter 1:14-15 NIV). 'Now that you have purified yourselves by obeying the truth so that you have sincere love for your brothers, love one another deeply, from the heart. *For* you have been born again, not of perishable seed, but of imperishable, through the living and enduring word of God' (1 Peter 1 22-23 NIV).

That seed makes such love possible because it enables all that is true of the Father in His relationship with Jesus to become true of us. 'Father, just as you are in me and I am in you. May they also be in us . . . . ' (John 17:21 NIV).

'I have given them the glory that you gave me, that they may be one as we are one. I in them and you in me' (John 17:22-23 NIV).

Much of 1 John is based on this concept:

'If you know that he is righteous you know that everyone who does what is right has been born of him' (1 John 2:29 NIV).

'We know that when he appears, we shall be like him, for we shall see him as he is' (1 John 3:2 NIV).

'He who does what is sinful is of the devil, because the devil has been sinning from the beginning. The reason the Son of God appeared was to destroy the devil's work. No-one who is born of God will continue to sin, because God's seed remains in him; he cannot go on sinning, because he has been born of God. This is how we know who the children of God are and who the children of the devil are: Anyone who does not do what is right is not a child of God; neither is anyone who does not love his brother' (1 John 3:8-10 NIV). This is a wonderful promise of progressive sanctification for the children of God. Many of us can testify to the power of His life. Sins which clung to us and beset us just a few years ago have had their grip upon us loosened and we have seen an ever-increasing measure of release. Look around and see the changes: angry, impatient brothers and sisters becoming more and more docile, happy and relaxed; critical, self-righteous saints having the sharp-edges beautifully rounded and softened; and hard, uncaring world-weary converts becoming vessels of love and renewal. This is the family likeness showing more and more.

'If anyone acknowledges that Jesus is the Son of God, God lives in him and he in God. And so we know and rely on the love God has for us. God is love. Whoever lives in love, lives in God, and God in him (1 John 4:15-16 NIV).

Hence John says 'Dear friends, let us love one another, for love comes from God. Everyone who loves has been born of God and knows God. Whoever does not love does not know God, because God is love' (1 John 4:7-8 NIV).

'If we love each other, God lives in us and his love is made complete in us' (1 John 4:12 NIV).

The Fatherhood of God is the key to all these truths. We have inherited the divine nature from Him with its unlimited potential for love, joy, peace, patience, kindness, goodness, faithfulness, gentleness and self-control. Furthermore we are children who 'listen to our Father's instruction' (Proverbs 1:8 NIV) and obey Him. Thus we come into the fullness of all that Jesus is.

Let us praise God that the laws of genetics which are so potent and dominant in our natural lives are a reflection of equally potent yet wonderfully simple laws wrought by Him in the spiritual realm. Hallelujah.

5

The Faith of God

The need for faith is constantly stressed in the New Testament. Not just 'saving faith' either, but the need for a continual day by day walk of faith by every believer. In Hebrews 11:6 we are told that 'without faith it is impossible to please God' (NIV) and this confirms the earlier statement that 'my righteous one will live by faith. And if he shrinks back, I will not be pleased with him' (Heb. 10:38 NIV).

From what we have seen so far it is quite clear that God has added a new dimension to the lives of those who have believed and put their trust in Him. But how important it is to see that the realities of the work He has performed come into our lives by the exercise of faith and by that alone. God tells us, for example, that by confessing our sins 'He is faithful and just and will forgive us our sins and purify us from all unrighteousness' (1 John 1:9 NIV). We have not an iota of proof that our sins will be removed or that our slate will be clean but we have faith that what He tells us is true, and as a result we confess our sins and believe His Word. Only then do we experience the forgiveness of sins and begin to walk in freedom. As the fruit follows the faith, it is obvious that where there is no faith there will be no fruit.

This applies in every area of our lives, but in none is it so important as the revelation of the new birth. It is no accident that when Jesus spoke to Nicodemus He drew a parallel between the new birth and the Exodus of Israel from Egypt, for the experience of the children of Israel has important lessons for us. The tragedy of Israel was that the glory of the Exodus was not followed by the liberty which God had purposed for them. Although God sent them directly north to the promised land, it was there, sitting on the border itself that the people began to doubt God's purpose and ability. Ten of the twelve spies sent out to collect information simply reflected the unbelieving attitude of the whole nation when they returned with a negative report. It was just what the people expected to hear.

The book of Hebrews gives a commentary on this. Referring to the Exodus generation the writer says '"Today, if you hear his voice, do not harden your hearts as you did in the rebellion" Who were they who heard and rebelled? Were they not all those Moses led out of Egypt? And with whom was he angry for forty years? Was it not with those who sinned, whose bodies fell in the desert? And to whom did God swear that they would never enter his rest, if not to those who disobeyed? *So we see that they were not able to enter, because of their unbelief*' (Heb. 3:15-18 NIV).

He goes further than this, however, and actually issues a warning to us. 'Therefore, since the promise of entering his rest still stands, let us be careful that none of you be found to have fallen short of it. For we also have had the gospel preached to us, just as they did; but the message they heard was of no value to them, *because those who heard did not combine it with faith*' (Heb. 4:1-2 NIV). A lack of faith robbed them of all God had prepared for them.

The incidents connected with this are recorded for us in the hope that we may actually learn something from history and not repeat their mistakes. Tragically many of God's people are just as unbelieving and faithless today, and as a result their experience is one of circling the wilderness like Israel did. It is still true that 'without faith it is *impossible* to please God' (Heb. 11:6 NIV).

It is not as though faith is in short supply either; believers and unbelievers live lives of faith every day. They trust the world and all the world's achievements totally. It is only with God that they have a problem. When we enter a building and walk upstairs we do not question for a moment whether the floor will be able to hold our weight. We believe implicitly that the architects have done their job correctly and that the builders have been diligent in following their instructions. We are sure that any floor, anywhere, can be walked upon with total peace of mind. We follow cooking instructions meticulously, we trust the doctor's diagnosis and his suggested remedy, and we believe that the water coming through our taps is drinkable. The trains marked 'Liverpool' will go to Liverpool, the banks really will give our money back to us, and so on. Why is it that with faith superabounding like this, it is so scarce towards God?

We Christians have got to learn that without faith we will never see the things of God being manifested in our lives. Indeed our spiritual family life will be at best impoverished, at worst destroyed unless we believe. That which God says He has done in us needs to be mixed with faith and put into action.

We sometimes hear people say about a certain brother or sister: 'Oh, he's a real doubting Thomas'. It is time that this was dropped from our vocabulary. The truth is that no believer can be described as a Thomas for when he was told that Jesus was alive, Thomas said 'Unless I see the nail marks in his hands and put my finger where the nails were, and put my hand into his side, I will not believe it.' (John 20:25 NIV). Very, very few of us have even seen Jesus, let alone touched Him, yet we have believed. Jesus says of all of us 'blessed are those who have not seen and yet have believed' (John 20:29 NIV). We start therefore from a higher point than Thomas[1].

Our problem, however, isn't our initial faith, it is our continuing faith. We are so used to walking by sight that we do not realise that the things God declares to be true of us are just as real and solid as those we can see, even though we may not at first be able to discern them. God demands that we exercise faith about these things.

Why is that? Why does God demand a life of faith?

It is quite simply because He has invested His Faith in us. I wonder how many of us have ever seen just how much faith God shows towards us. It is revealed in some of the things God says of us. It was pure faith on God's part when He decided to call those of us who have put their trust in Him BELIEVERS. Even though many doubts and distinct periods of unbelief creep in, God still insists that we are believers!

He calls all believers SAINTS. Carnal, out-of-fellowship, even downright sinful believers are still called saints. The Church at Corinth has been described as the 'Las Vegas of the Ancient World', and Paul writes his letters to them to castigate them for their sinful way. But how does he begin his letter? 'To the church of God in Corinth, to those sanctified in Christ Jesus and called to be holy . . . . ' (1 Cor. 1:2 NIV). He writes it under the anointing of the Holy Spirit too, and it represents tremendous faith. God will not have them known in any other way.

All believers are called kings and priests. 1 Peter 2:9 clearly states it: 'But you are a chosen people, a royal

---

1. Thomas went on to establish 1500 churches in India.

priesthood, a holy nation, a people belonging to God.' He declares the belief that we reign in life and are actively functioning before Him, and uses it of everyone, no matter what spiritual state they are in.

We are all called OVERCOMERS. 'For everyone born of God has overcome the world. This is the victory that has overcome the world, even our faith. Who is it that overcomes the world? Only he who believes that Jesus is the Son of God' (1 John 5:4-5 NIV). This, of course, includes every believer whether or not they believe it or experience it. God knows that Christ has won the outright victory for us all and 'always leads us in triumphal procession in Christ' (2 Cor. 2:14 NIV). It is no accident that the description of Christ's return in Revelation 19:11-16 shows the armies following Jesus dressed in 'linen, white and clean' (v14 NIV). They do no fighting because Jesus has done it all. He leads them in victory.

We are called 'Witnesses', 'Ambassadors for Christ', 'Citizens of Heaven'. These are titles of faith and apply to all who are born again whether they are actively evangelical or silent.

There are many more examples, too. We are called the 'Church' – a Greek word which means 'the called out ones' – 'the Body of Christ', with the implication that we are as holy, selfless and glorifying to the Father as Jesus was. Even our 'unity' is a matter of faith. Ephesians 4:3 does not tell us to 'make the unity of the Spirit' but 'to keep the unity of the Spirit'. As far as God is concerned the Body of Jesus was split once on the Cross, never to be divided again. It is FAITH, FAITH, FAITH.

Most of us would never have been so faith-filled. Knowing what the believers at Corinth and many other places were like we would have expressed things very differently. 'To the doubters of Galatia' or 'to the so-called saints of Corinth' would have sprung readily from our lips. We seem to have a natural tendency to walk in what we call 'reality'—that which *is* not—instead of faith.

God doesn't speak in this way because He reckons that His work, the work He has achieved in us, is more real, more powerful and more permanent than anything else, even our present experience. Indeed He is the God 'who gives life to the dead and calls *things that are not as though they were*' (Romans 4:17 NIV). We must imitate Him and follow in His example.

If more believers did, they would find the transformation of their lives occurring very rapidly. The problem is often sheer ignorance—they just do not fully know what God has done in their lives and are not really persuaded about what they do know. They are fully convinced about the old life and its power and potency. Indeed most believers have been dominated and kicked around by it for many, many years. But the truth is that it doesn't compare with the power of the new.

The birth process itself clearly shows this. When a baby is born six miracles[1] occur:

1. The blood flow changes direction.
2. The hole between the two upper chambers of the heart begins to close.
3. The duct between the aorta and the pulmonary artery closes.
4. The umbilical arteries contract and the ends gradually become ligaments.
5. The umbilical vein closes and becomes a ligament.
6. The ductus venosus (an important vein carrying oxygenated blood) closes and also becomes a ligament in time.

1. I am grateful to my wife for this information.

But when a person is born-again many more than six miracles occur — I have counted 37[1] so far and there are many more. To name just a few of them:-

We are forgiven all our sins (Eph. 1:7).
We are made acceptable to God (Eph. 1:6).
We are brought near to God (Eph. 2:13 and 19).
We are declared righteous (Romans 3:24).
We are born of God (John 3:7).
We are created anew (2 Cor. 5:17).
We are delivered from the powers of darkness (Col. 1:13).
We are transferred into God's kingdom (Col. 1:13).
We are made joint-heirs with Christ (Romans 8:17).
We are united with Father, Son and Holy Spirit
(1Thess. 1:1) (John 14:20)

Natural birth is totally eclipsed by the supernatural one.

So surely the new nature has more power than the old. If it doesn't, then we are believing that the first Adam from whom we received the old, is more powerful than the last Adam (Jesus) from whom we have received the new. That is utterly wrong.

Paul in Romans 12:2 said 'Do not conform any longer to the pattern of this world, but be transformed by the renewing of your mind. Then *you* will be able to test and approve what God's will is — his good, pleasing and perfect will' (NIV).

The 'transformation' occurs through the renewing of our minds. When we start receiving new information, dwelling on it and believing it changes start occurring. The word 'transformation' is the Greek word 'metamorphoo' from

---

1. Listed on my tape 'Functioning in the Church' BBS 102.
   Available from 'Tapes' 30, Crescent Road, Bognor Regis, PO21 1QG.
   A similar list of 50 is given in the Victor Bible Source Book (Scripture Press).

which we get our word 'metamorphosis'. A metamorphosed substance looks different from the original material. Graphite is one form of carbon – diamond is another. It is the same basic material, but in a totally different structure.

So what Paul is saying is that if we can really get to grips with what God has done in our lives, although we'll be the same recognizable person, we will be dramatically altered. The same word is used at the Transfiguration of Jesus. As Peter, James and John looked on, Jesus, who had walked up the mountain with them was changed before their eyes: 'He was transfigured before them. His face shone like the sun, and his clothes became as white as the light' (Matth. 17:2 NIV). They knew it was still Jesus, but He had changed. Years later Peter was to recall this incident and say of it that they had seen the Lord as He would be at the Second Advent. 'We did not follow cleverly invented stories when we told you about the power and coming of our Lord Jesus Christ, but we were eyewitnesses of his majesty' (2 Peter 1:16 NIV). He had been metamorphosed.

The new man in us is the power of our transformation. There is an initial revelation of the new man in our lives, with more and more being revealed as our lives progress.

My father was dumbfounded when I first visited home for a weekend after my conversation. I tried desperately to pluck up courage and tell him about all that Jesus had done for me, and to witness to the fact that Jesus was alive from the dead, but I didn't seem able to do it – words failed me; openings seemed to be unnatural and finally I retired in defeat.

It was my father who then forced the issue into the open. Coming to sit with me on the Sunday afternoon, he gazed at me for some time and finally got up and switched off the music I was listening to. After a few more minutes' silence he then said 'What on earth has happened to you? Not only are you peaceful and happy – you look different.' It was true, and I was able to tell him of the new birth. The frightened, depressed son who had left home a few months before had come home a new person.

Since that time I have seen more and more clearly just how different the new creation is from the old which had dominated me for so many years. As I launched out, it was thrilling to find that I could do the things which God's word said I could do. He had given me a new heart of love and I could love; He had given me the Holy Spirit so I could move and live uprightly in this fallen world; He had brought me near to God, so that I could show the glory which accompanies those who live under His canopy of love.

The first step for us all is to believe. God has done wonderful, dynamic things in us and He wants us to have faith so that they might be revealed. Romans 12:2 ends by saying that after our minds are renewed, we 'will be able to test and approve what God's will is' (NIV). It will be seen in us.

As Peter kept his eyes on Jesus he was able to do the impossible and walk upon the troubled waters. He continued, but only until he lost sight of Jesus and the waves and wind became more real to him. Yet even when he failed, Jesus was there to save him.

The Lord wants us to walk on the waters of our former lives – believing that we are newly born and enabled to live as God wants – knowing that even if we fail He is there to help us again. As we do this we will see the glory of the Lord shining through us.

The power at work within us is enough to accomplish this, for as Jesus said in Mark 4:26-28 'This is what the kingdom of God is like. A man scatters seed on the ground. Night and day, whether he sleeps or gets up, the seed sprouts and grows, though he does not know how. All by itself the soil produces corn – first the stalk, then the ear, then the full kernel in the ear' (NIV).

The new life will grow. It takes time, but it has the power of God in it and its eventual fruitfulness is beyond question. The course of our lives is the greenhouse for its development.

6

Growing Up in God

'Make the most of it, it won't last long'. My aunt spoke with the voice of experience. 'They'll be leaving school before you know what has happened.'

She is right, of course. Time, our constant enemy, passes by very rapidly and there is nothing like the growth and development of children to bring it forcibly home to us. Stage follows stage with such relentlessness and rapidity it can leave one breathless. The joys and problems of one stage of childhood soon make way for the fresh joys and problems of the next.

I still relish the happiness and freedom I felt when at long last my wife and I no longer needed to take the two nappy buckets with us every time we went away; or the happy day when the stair gate could safely be removed. What a relief too, when instead of putting all breakables on the highest shelf out of the way, and having to warn others to do the same, they could be put back into their rightful places. The children were growing up fast.

Growing up occurs both in the natural and the spiritual life. The major difference is, however, that while one occurs automatically with all children arriving at the same point of physical development within a year or two of one anothers, the other varies enormously from person to person. A Christian's development does not depend on how long he has been saved but on how much teaching he has received and how devoted and fervent he has been. One believer of ten years' standing may still be a nappy-bound babe in Christ, another may be already tackling the steak. Unfortunately we have to admit that there are many more immature Christians around in the Church today than mature ones and this is a major weakness.

Perhaps the mental, educational and behavioural development of a child more closely parallels a Christian's development. One of the research projects I undertook at University examined the role of the home in educational attainment. Not surprisingly I found that the parental attitude and input was absolutely crucial in the education of a child. A less intelligent child constantly helped and motivated at home was likely to make much more progress than a more intelligent child from a home where no interest was shown, no discussion occurred and where the television was allowed to blot out all else. Educational equality is a 'pipe-dream' in such circumstances.

We as Christian parents must realize that the Bible not only puts the responsibility of bringing up our children in 'the nurture and admonition of the Lord' (Eph. 6:4) on our shoulders (no Sunday school teacher can possibly do what we are neglecting to do), but it also says that we have a crucial part to play in the teaching of basic skills. 'Listen, my son, to your father's instruction and do not forsake your mother's teaching' (Prov. 1:8 NIV) refers to the whole of life, not just spiritual education.

What the parent does in a child's development, the Word of God is designed to do in a believer's life. In the early Church the believers 'devoted themselves to the apostles' teaching and to the fellowship, to the breaking of bread and to prayer' (Acts 2:42 NIV). 2 Timothy 3:16 says 'All Scripture is God-breathed and is useful for teaching, rebuking, correcting and training in righteousness' and its aim is described as being 'that the man of God may be thoroughly equipped for every good work' (NIV). The Word teaches, rebukes, corrects and trains in righteousness, and these four tasks also perfectly sum up the ministry of a parent. We teach basic skills, rebuke where there is wrong-doing and give the positive correction. Our lives should give an example of uprightness and godliness. The 'do what I say, not as I do' principle practised by so many today is a recipe for disaster. It is worth noting that many children fail to go on with God because they see a lack of genuine devotion in their parents' lives at home. They hear criticism, gossip and evil-speaking about other Christians around the dinner table, and yet see their parents apparently relating happily with these people in church the next day. They see praise and the Bible being read on Sundays, but nothing like that happens in the living room. Their conclusion is that Christians are hypocrites and it engenders rebellion and lack of respect in them. It is a warning we must all heed.

The Word of God is the daily diet of the believer – milk at first, and meat later on – and it provides all that is needed for steady maturing. A diligent intake of the Word, preferably in the setting of a thriving Christian community, will ensure rapid growth. Full maturity does take time – as the Arabs say, 'no matter how great the heat, a block of ice won't melt instantly' – but it need not take as long as we might assume. There is no excuse for 20 year-old-converts still being babes.

Such slow growth is rebuked firmly in the Bible. The writer to the Hebrews criticized his readers most strongly for their immaturity, and any Bible teacher knows the frustration he felt . . . . 'We have much to say about this, but it is hard to explain because you are slow to learn. In fact, though by this time you ought to be teachers, you need someone to teach you the frustration he felt . . . .

77

'We have much to say about this, but it is hard to explain because you are slow to learn. In fact, though by this time you ought to be teachers, you need someone to teach you the elementary truths of God's Word all over again. You need milk, not solid food. Anyone who lives on milk, being still an infant, is not acquainted with teaching about righteousness. But solid food is for the mature, who by constant use have trained themselves to distinguish good from evil' (Hebrews 5:11-14 NIV).

These believers were old enough to have become teachers, but they were still babes. As a result the writer says that he could not give them the steak of the Word, but had to bottle-feed them instead. I have often experienced this and have longed to launch into the details and glories of the text only to be met by a group of people hoping for a 20 minute sermonette. How I long to see days like the times of Paul, when he hired the lecture hall of Tyrannus and for two years taught the believers every afternoon while the town enjoyed its siesta. (See Acts 19:9). I realize that it would not be universally popular with most Christians today.

The result of being a babe is that while the old nature inherited from our natural parents is full-grown, the nature inherited spiritually from the Father in heaven is often under-developed, restricted and weak. It shows in outward behaviour, for a child always acts like a child. The Corinthian believers were castigated by Paul in these terms: 'Brothers, I could not address you as spiritual but as worldly – mere infants in Christ. I gave you milk, not solid food, for you were not yet ready for it. Indeed, you are still not ready. You are still worldly. For since there is jealously and quarrelling among you, are you not worldly? Are you not acting like mere men?' (1 Cor. 3:1-3 NIV). 'Acting like mere men' is the description of a babe in Christ's behaviour. It is impossible to distinguish between the way they act and the way unbelievers act. All you need is a church filled with these babes, and gossip, division, personality clashes and in-fighting will be the norm. More energy is spent trying to keep peace and unity in the Church today than is spent advancing the Gospel. That is the disgrace of our age. The answer to it is that we must grow up.

The Bible gives us an indication of this growing up process. 'The Greeks had a word for it' is a well-known saying and it was coined because of the accuracy of the Greek language. English is a fine language, but New Testament Greek exceeds it in richness and detail. Not for the Greeks just one word for love; they had four (agape, phileo, eros and charis), and all with distinct and definite meanings. Nor did they have only one word for 'another', but because they realized that it could be used in two different ways i.e. 'another' of the same kind; and 'another' of a different kind, they had two. Paul used both in Galatians 1:6-7: 'I marvel that ye are so soon removed from him that called you unto the grace of Christ into another (Heteros = another of a different kind) gospel: which is not another (ALLOS = another of the same kind)' i.e. 'They preach a totally different Gospel, don't ever think that it is even similar'. This is an indication of how accurate a language it is.

It is not surprising then that the different stages of development are described by using different words. We can list these[1]:-

1. PAIDION = An infant which has just been born
2. NEPIOS = the word actually means 'without the power of speech', and denotes a child under 2 years of age.

---

1. This first came to my attention in an article by Ralph Mahoney, in the New Zealand 'Logos' Magazine Vol. 3 Dec. 1969.

3. TEKNION = a little child. It is the diminutive form of TEKNON and is often used as a term of affection.

4. TEKNON = a young child. Because it is from the word TIKTO='to give birth to' it emphasizes our relationship with our parents.

5. HUIOS = a mature son.

These are stages we can all recognize in our own children's growth – all children pass through these, and if all goes well, by the age of eighteen to twenty they come into full maturity. God wants to see his children pass successfully and swiftly through these stages too, but as we have seen, it depends on the determination and free-will of the individual concerned.

We can examine **Paidion**, **Nepios** and **Teknion** together. A baby or young child lives entirely in a world of the senses. It tastes, touches, feels, hears and sees. It knows nothing of self-restraint or discipline but is completely self-centred and self-occupied. If it wants something, then it will make as much fuss and noise as is necessary to get what it wants. As it cannot communicate with any accuracy the fuss continues until the desired end is achieved. If this means waking up the parents in the night, or refusing to be 'put down' for the usual afternoon nap, so be it. No matter how important the visitor, or how grand the occasion, the child's self-will is paramount. 'At least he's got a good pair of lungs' has been used time without number to cover parental embarrassment. Let Christian parents understand fully that the training of children must begin at this early age, for often the pattern of behaviour instigated at that age determines what happens later. I am convinced that a baby tries to train its parents from the day it is born. If it is bored at

3.00 am then Mummy and Daddy must be trained to come and entertain it. Many parents learn the lessons only too well, and often within a year are desperately trying to break out of the mould.

A child of this age doesn't mind who he (or she) disturbs. When he makes a mess he is totally oblivious of what he has done or of the work others will have to do to clear it up. He can be seen lying in the scene of disaster chuckling happily and blowing bubbles of joy.

If he had his way he would be picked up and carried all the time, and never would responsibility be placed on his shoulders. If it were possible, everything would be done for him all the time. He likes all the things that are bad for him – anything sweet, as often as possible please; and dust, mud and insects whenever available. The mouth is the centre of feeling and so everything is pushed into it. The things that are good for him – meat and two veg., or the morning's Weetabix – go on the floor or on the head! He tries to do 'his own thing' all the time, and he makes even more fuss if he is ever denied or corrected.

We all know believers like this, and certainly all of us who have been born again have been through this stage. Let those of us who are mature not frown at those who are genuinely going through this period. It is easy for older Christians to forget what they were like at that age.

I clearly remember a teacher colleague of mine applying such double standards. He was always boasting what a rebellious, difficult child he had been when he was at school and laughing at the problems he had caused. Yet the same man would come in and berate and moan about first year pupils for being difficult when he was trying to line them up at the bus stop after school!!

How I praise God for the love and endless patience that the believers showed me as I was passing through this stage. How they put up with me I do not know, and I'm sure there were times when they secretly wished God had saved an easier character. Fortunately I grew rapidly through this phase.

Paul, as we have seen, rebuked older believers who were still exhibiting these behavioural traits. I know many believers who, while old in terms of years are still in this stage – they do what they want all the time, kick up a fuss if they are not being pampered, and always insist on being right or justified. They need constant, overt expressions of love and if these are not forthcoming they are likely to sulk or accuse their Christian group of being unloving. Very often that means that others must greet them in a meeting and notice them, but of course they have no such responsibility to others. They can never be corrected in any way without a big scene or fuss. They are always right (of course) and though immature themselves, know exactly what is wrong with everyone else. They think they are the most spiritual, most faith-filled and most neglected of believers and in their keenness they don't notice the mess, trouble and hurt they are causing on every side.

I repeat, that in the newly-converted, these things are expected, but when a twenty-year-old is still doing them there is something very wrong indeed.

Teknon

Hopefully, with babyhood successfully negotiated, the youngster then ploughs on. Often this period begins with a calm, stable phase in which Christianity is pleasant and relaxed. However, the teenage storm often follows.

At this point one of two things may occur, and sometimes both. The first is that often the old life reappears on the scene and the devil tempts the youngster. When Joshua and his army had defeated Jericho, they marched on towards Bethel ('The house of God') but found Ai was first on the route. 'Ai' means 'a heap' or 'the rubbish tip' and I have often thought how it represents our old life. Some suffer a temporary defeat here, and God uses it to expose some hidden, undealt-with area. In 1 John 2:16 all sin is said to belong to one of three categories: 'For all that is in the world, the lust of the flesh, and the lust of the eyes, and the pride of life, is not of the Father, but is of the world.'

When Jesus was tempted by the devil, it is significant that He was tested three times, once in each of these areas.

(a) The temptation to turn stones into bread, which was the lust of the flesh.
(b) The temptation to cast Himself down from the pinnacle of the temple, which was the pride of life.
(c) The temptation of receiving all the kingdoms of the world, which was the lust of the eyes.

Jesus resisted all of these despite being 'tempted in every way, just as we are'. (Heb. 4:15 NIV). So He can understand our situation and 'is not ashamed to call us brothers' (Heb. 2:11 NIV).

At Ai, Achan's hidden sin was fully exposed. He had hidden three things – a Babylonish garment, a golden bust, and money. Again these relate to the same three categories of sin:

(a) The Babylonish garment   – lust of the eyes.
(b) The golden bust   – pride of life.
(a) Money   – lust of the flesh.

As the believer approaches his spiritual teenage years, the reality of sin and its horrors is often exposed, and hidden areas come up which need to be dealt with.

This is sometimes followed by, or sometimes is eclipsed altogether by, a period of high-powered, energized devotion to the Lord. The available energy knows no bounds and is poured into the faith. The Bible defines this period well when it says 'The glory of young men is their strength, grey hair the splendour of the old' (Proverbs 20:29 NIV). This is really a contrast – the energy of the young versus the wisdom of the older person.

The teenage Christian cannot imagine why other believers are so slow and fuddy-duddy. When he prays every prayer is answered immediately, or if it isn't there is a greater glory in the explanation of why it wasn't. Every mountain becomes a mole-hill; every day they 'run through a troop and leap over a wall' (from Psalm 18:29) and the Lord's voice is clear and direct. It is vital that older Christians do not feel threatened by this stage or by the frantic energy which accompanies it. They must not try to curb it wrongly. Maturity will soon add wisdom to it, and hopefully a balance will be achieved. Certainly the difficulties of the Christian life will come soon enough and so it is important that they are allowed to enjoy this stage and use it, for often a firm foundation is laid in this period which will stand them in good stead.

The great problem of this period is pride and its accompanying intolerance. This is why Paul insisted that an elder 'must not be a recent convert, or he may become conceited and fall under the same judgment as the devil' (1 Tim. 3:6 NIV). Obviously a person being considered for eldership is a keen, growing individual, and if he is a new convert he is likely to be in his 'teenage' period. I believe there is a warning here which believers should heed. It happens all too often that a very young believer with a good testimony is put into the pulpit and launched into a ministry long before he or she is ready for it. The results are usually disastrous. Either the so-called minister runs out of things to say and dries up spiritually; or he ministers in pride and rushes in 'where angels fear to tread'. Either way he will have a very hard time and may end up damaged, isolated or bitter. Worse still, he or she may damage or unknowingly mislead immature believers. The Bible is as always absolutely right, and we ignore it at our peril.

I was totally insufferable in this stage, but fortunately I was surrounded at University by others in the same position. We were only a threat to those older, wiser student believers who could, thankfully for them, escape from us. We had a glorious time. I have to say that I was the noisiest, most unruly, most dogmatic and arrogant of them all. How gracious God was to us. We all called one another 'brother' and 'sister' all the time and shouted 'Praise the Lord' and 'Hallelujah' at the slightest provocation (raising eyebrows all round the liberated student body). I still shudder when I remember that everyone called me 'bro'! After lectures we gathered to share the latest from heaven and to come together for another prayer meeting. If a sudden difficulty and burden were to arise then one or two car loads of us would set off for the hills nearby so that we could seek the Lord and pray. Usually we returned at 2.00 or 3.00 am although sometimes we didn't reappear until breakfast next morning. No one was too much trouble, time was limitless and all other Christians had to be prayed into our fervour and devotion. Why didn't they see it as we did?

They were wonderful, not-to-be-missed, days and I don't regret one of them. The sheer joy of finding that you *had* heard the Lord's voice. I remember travelling around Leicester Square in a friend's car (pre-pedestrianization) and suddenly knowing that I had to speak to two men who were standing together by a shop. 'Stop the car' I shouated, and jumping out and running towards them said 'Do you want to know about Jesus Christ?' 'We've just been talking about it' they said. We took them to the cafeteria of the Royal Festival Hall, and after an hour or so both were wonderfully converted. We didn't even know their names, but as we drove off we left two dazed, but radiant children of God, drunk in the Spirit, dancing back to their homes.

What gratitude I have in my heart though to those more mature believers whose fellowships I have visited, who moulded and directed me without destroying the fervent devotion. The endless hospitality shown to me, the cost and effort of which hardly crossed my mind. Selfish, loud but glorious days. The responsibilities of a job and a family came soon enough, and I still relish the lessons I learned in those days and the miracles I experienced. In reality my life was still a shambles, but it was as if 'the times of this ignorance God winked at' (Acts 17:30).

While the inevitable youthful pride is dented sooner or later, much more serious is the possibility of getting into error and false doctrine at this time. Researchers say that the sects pick up people who are mainly between the ages of 18 and 24, and that this age-range represents one of the most vulnerable periods of life. Only solid Bible teaching and knowledge can stop this and this is why it is essential that babes in Christ who are fed milk at first are soon weaned onto the solids. Truth in the inward parts from an early age is the best defence against error in later years. The 'elementary teachings about Christ' (Heb. 6:1 NIV) must be in place as early as possible.

Before going on to the fifth word 'HUIOS' it is helpful to understand something of God's dealings with us and with those who are less mature. We must first accept that it is just not possible for 'an old head to be put on young shoulders' – all we would succeed in doing is bringing young believers into bondage and be seen as religious or legalistic ourselves. Rather, we must understand the grace of God and stop ourselves being critical or intolerant.

We can represent each believer's life by a grid of dots in which each dot is an area of sin or error which God wants to deal with. If we then represent the believer with a circle which becomes ever larger the more he or she matures, we find an interesting result.

A Young Believer

Here only one area of the life is being pointed at by God and the believer has to deal with that area alone.

A 'Teenage Believer'

As the believer grows the circle expands and so the area of conviction has enlarged. More and more areas are now under God's scrutiny and hence the believer is conscious of God's increasing conviction in his life.

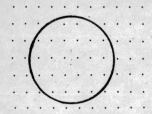 Many areas of God's dealing

A mature believer may see another less mature believer getting away with many things that he himself is convicted of and punished for, and sometimes he may feel aggrieved about this. But it is the natural process of growing up, and the mature believer must not forget the grace showered upon him when he was young.

After all, we don't severely discipline a six-month-old baby when he tips up his dinner and it goes all over the floor, but if a 12 year old does the same he will certainly receive discipline, hot and strong. God deals with us on the same basis. Praise Him that He does, or none of us would ever be able to grow at all in the Christian life.

But what about the believers who have left the elementary stages and who come under the title HUIOS – those who are mature and developed? The truth about them is so glorious that we must develop it at length.

Let us praise God that one day we will all be mature sons for as Ephesians 1:5 says 'he predestined us to be adopted as his sons (HUIOS) through Jesus Christ, in accordance with his pleasure and will' (NIV). We are all going to make it!

1. I am grateful to Dr Charles Clough for the basic idea here.

7

Adoption

So far we have seen the development of a child through the early and middle stages of growth – the stages the Greeks defined with the use of the words Paidion, Nepios, Teknion and Teknon. It is easy to assume that the last word, HUIOS, is simply the final stage in development, at which a youth becomes a mature adult. That is not the case.

In Israel and in many other ancient cultures the word 'son' or 'HUIOS' had a very important and specific meaning[1]. If a person was introduced as His father's 'son' (HUIOS), then everyone knew that he held a very highly regarded place in his father's esteem and was totally trusted by him.

A man might have five sons all aged between 20 and 30 but it could be that only two of the five would bear the title of 'HUIOS' or 'SON'. It was not dependent on age but on experience and trustworthiness. If you bore the designation 'SON' it meant that your father totally trusted your judgment and that as far as he was concerned your word was as binding and powerful as if he himself had given it. He knew that you thought the same way as he did, had the same goals and concerns as he did, and that your assessment of any given situation was as

1. 'Logos' Magazine Vol. 3. Dec. 1969.

accurate as his. As a result he could, for example, send you to market, knowing that the animals you bought would be the best and that had you sold any animals you would have got the most favourable price possible.

In modern terms it would be equivalent of instructing your bank manager to allow your son's signature to pass on your cheques. Certainly when business was done with a man's son it was as binding as if the negotiations had been conducted by the man himself.

Obviously no man would give a foolish, unreliable or spendthrift boy the chance of squandering his money because 'a fool and his money are soon parted' and so the title 'HUIOS' or 'SON' was used very carefully indeed. Everyone in the community knew who your 'SON' was and which of your boys were allowed to use that title. Conversely they would also know who could not. To ensure that there was no confusion a public ceremony was held and the townsfolk all turned out to witness it. The father would take a boy who had proved himself able and devoted and proudly march with him down to the market square. There he would put his son onto a step or stone and call the crowds to gather around. He would then declare in a loud voice: 'This is my son (HUIOS).' This conferred on the boy the legal rights and honour due to the father himself. All the witnesses knew from that time on that when they dealt with the son they were in effect dealing with the father.

This ceremony was called 'HUIOTHESIA' by the Greeks. It is from two Greek words 'tithemi' = 'to place' and 'huios' = 'an adult son' and is literally 'placing a son'. In our New Testament 'HUIOTHESIA' is used five times and is translated every time by the word 'ADOPTION'.

This is the source of much confusion today because the word 'Adoption' has another meaning in contemporary society. So it is important that we distinguish carefully between the Biblical use of the word and our present day use. If you 'adopt' a child today you take the necessary action to make someone else's son or daughter – a child not physically related to you at all – legally your own. Once the difficult process has been successfully negotiated such children grow up as if they were your own and use your surname, while in fact they are genetically and physically totally different from you.

I have heard a parallel drawn between this legal process and our adoption by God, which sometimes gives the impression that our relationship with God is a legal one only. As we know from our studies so far that is not true – we are not just legally related to our heavenly Father, we have actually been born to Him and He really is our Father. We are His children and have the seed of God Himself within us. So it is obvious that when the New Testament talks of our adoption it is not the modern sense of the word the writers have in mind, but the ancient practice of 'placing a son'. As W.E. Vine in his *Expository Dictionary of New Testament Words*[1] says, 'God does not adopt believers as children. They are begotten as such by His Holy Spirit through faith. Adoption is a term involving the dignity of the relationship of believers as sons; it is not a putting into the family by spiritual birth, but a putting into the position of sons.'

While it is something we will all eventually come into (Eph. 1:5) our lives on this Earth are part of the training for that time. Adam failed in this. When he was tested his will was found to be against God – his sin was that he refused to obey God's command. He failed therefore to achieve sonship. But where Adam failed Jesus succeeded.

1. W. E. Vine *Expository Dictionary of New Testament Words*. Marshall Morgan & Scott. p32.

The writer of the letter to the Hebrews says that 'In bringing many sons to glory, it was fitting that God, for whom and through whom everything exists, should make the Pioneer of their salvation perfect through suffering' (Heb. 2:10 NIV). This is not denying the sinlessness of Jesus; what it *is* saying is that Jesus too had His will tested but, unlike Adam, remained loyal to His Father through every test. After thirty years of life on the Earth Jesus had shown Himself worthy by constantly choosing to go His Father's way. He was a person after His Father's own heart.

As a result, when Jesus was thirty years of age, God the Father took him through the ceremony of adoption. Before this time Jesus lived and worked as a carpenter, but was unrecognized and as far as we know performed no miracles at all. Then, on God's chosen day, Jesus joined the throng who gathered around John the Baptist. John's message was very clear. 'I baptize with water . . . but among you stands one you do not know. He is the one who comes after me, the thongs of whose sandals I am not worthy to untie' (John 1:26-27 NIV). The narrative then continues: 'The next day John saw Jesus coming towards him and said, "Look, the Lamb of God, who takes away the sin of the world! This is the one I meant when I said, 'A man who comes after me has surpassed me because he was before me'"' (John 1:29-30 NIV).

Despite John's protest Jesus went into the water and was baptized by him. As He came up from the water two things occurred: the Spirit of God came upon Him, and God spoke. 'As soon as Jesus was baptized, he went up out of the water. At that moment heaven was opened, and he saw the Spirit of God descending like a dove and lighting on him. And a voice from heaven said, "This is my Son (HUIOS), whom I love; with him I am well pleased"' (Matt. 3:16-17 NIV).

Here was a public adoption ceremony: our heavenly Father making the pronouncement that Jesus was trusted by Him, having proved His devotion by His life-long service.

Jesus' baptism mirrors very closely a Roman adoption ceremony.[1] When a Roman child was young his father made sure that he had the best education available and very firm discipline. Often cultured Greek captives would be put in charge of the teenage boys, and the children learned from them much that Greece had to teach. Those who excelled and who impressed their families and tutors with their responsible, self-controlled, mature behaviour were chosen to go through the adoption ceremony. They were taken to the Forum, introduced to the people and then the father read a proclamation to the effect that he was delighted with his boy and from now on counted him a son (HUIOS). Then the father gave his son a long robe called the TOGA VIRILIS which he would wear from that time on to signify his new status. He immediately received part of his inheritance (the rest came later); he was allowed to manage his own affairs and he could speak on behalf of his father.

So we see the pattern of Jesus' Baptism. Jesus was God's 'only begotten Son'. At this ceremony He received the empowering of the Holy Spirit—it was His TOGA VIRILIS—and the Father testified to the world that He was delighted with Him and henceforth considered Him a mature son (HUIOS).

This declaration was soon followed by a public demonstration of that new authority. Once He had been baptized Jesus' ministry began in earnest—indeed He gave up all carpentry and spent the remaining three and a half years going 'through all the towns and villages

1. See F. R. Cowell *Everyday Life in Ancient Rome*. Batsford/Putnam. p. 128.

teaching in their synagogues, preaching the good news of the kingdom and healing every kind of disease and sickness' (Matt. 9:35 NIV). He used His heavenly Father's name and authority to heal the sick and rebuke demons.

Jesus spoke of His ministry in a very specific way in terms of His adoption.

'I have come in my Father's name' (John 5:43 NIV).

'So Jesus said, "When you have lifted up the Son of Man, then you will know who I am and that I do nothing on my own but speak just what the Father has taught me"' (John 8:28 NIV).

'I must work the works of him that sent me' (John 9:4)

'I no longer call you servants, because a servant does not know his master's business. Instead, I have called you friends, for everything that I learned from my Father I have made known to you' (John 15:15 NIV).

In all this Jesus became the perfect Son. Though He was Himself God and therefore sovereign, omnipotent, omnipresent and omniscient, yet He laid these attributes aside so that He would work not His own works, but those of His Father.

'Who, being in very nature God, did not consider equality with God something to be grasped, but made himself nothing, taking the very nature of a servant, being made in human likeness. And being found in appearance as a man, he humbled himself and became obedient to death – even death on a cross!

Therefore God exalted him to the highest place and gave him the name that is above every name, that at the name of Jesus every knee should bow, in heaven and on earth and under the earth, and every tongue confess that Jesus Christ is Lord, to the glory of God the Father' (Phil. 2:6-11 NIV).

This glorious calling is also ours. We might be weak,

but God has given us His power and ability. Not only have we received the Holy Spirit, which in Romans 8:15 is called 'the Spirit of adoption', but His purpose in our lives is to see that we all reach the place where 'we might receive the full rights of sons' (Gal. 4:5 NIV). That we will reach it is not open to question, for 'he predestined us to be adopted as his sons' (Eph. 1:5 NIV). Rather we must ask what we can do to further God's purpose in our lives. He has called us 'SONS': how do we live and walk as sons?

Before answering this it is vital that we see some of the other glories associated with Sonship.

8

The Essence of Sonship

So far we have examined the Fatherhood and family of God, and traced the development of God's children through to full mature sonship. So glorious is God's plan that He has determined to have a whole family of mature sons and the work of Jesus has achieved all that is necessary to bring 'many sons to glory' (Hebrews 2:10 NIV).

As we have already seen, we have to get out of our minds the western idea that the word 'son' (HUIOS) means any male child in a family. That was certainly not how people understood it at the time of Jesus, for the word 'son' carried with it a recognition of maturity, authority and of dignity. When it appears in the New Testament it is said to be the aim of God for all believers, male and female. Indeed He has already designated us 'SONS' because He knows that His work will come to fruition. As Paul wrote: 'being confident of this, that he who began a good work in you will carry it on to completion . . . . ' (Phil. 1:6 NIV).

As both male and female believers are included in this it might be asked why God retained the title 'Sonship' and didn't replace it with 'daughterhood' or some 'non-sexist' expression. We might also ask why the Bible is so insistent that God is always seen as a Father and why Jesus is male.

It is important that we get the apostate, rebellious

thinking of the world out of our heads, and think biblically about this. Adam and Eve were both created by God, but God decided to make Adam first and then Eve. Indeed Eve was given to him as the perfect partner for the task he had to do in Eden. Genesis is very clear about this. 'The LORD God took the man and put him in the Garden of Eden to work it and take care of it' (Gen. 2:15 NIV) and 'The LORD God said, "It is not good for the man to be alone. I will make a helper suitable for him"' (Gen. 2:18 NIV). The paradise in Eden gave Adam and Eve a relaxed, meaningful and fulfilled existence, but even before the Fall there was a male-female divide and the male came first. 'For man did not come from woman, but woman from man; neither was man created for woman, but woman for man' (1 Cor. 11:8-9 NIV).

At the Fall, male and female played different parts, for whereas Eve was deceived the Bible clearly states that it was Adam who deliberately rebelled against God and thereby brought the Fall into the world. Adam's decision to eat was all the worse because undoubtedly he could see what effect his disobedience would have when he looked at the already fallen Eve. She had after all, eaten the fruit first and suffered the consequences[1] Adam's action was deliberate and premeditated.

So it is that the whole of the New Testament insists that the Fall is Adam's fault, not Eve's and that he is the one who passed on the effects to us all. 'Sin entered the world through one man, and death through sin, and in this way death came to all men' (Romans 5:12 NIV); 'By the trespass of the one man, death reigned .... ' (Romans 5:17 NIV). Eve is not named for she was deceived in her ignorance.

1. There is an implication in the Bible that Adam and Eve were clothed with light before the Fall. The moment Eve ate of the fruit, she would have lost this covering.

Because of this historical order of events the male is seen as the instigator, and the one who passes on an inheritance: indeed the Fall is still passed on to us from Adam through the male parent. This is one of the reasons – though not the only one[1] – why the virgin birth of Jesus was necessary. He had to be untainted by the Fall of man.

Because of this, Jesus had to be a man. 'For if, by the trespass of the one man, death reigned through that one man, how much more will those who receive God's abundant provision of grace and of the gift of righteousness reign in life through the one man, Jesus Christ' (Romans 5:17 NIV).

'For just as through the disobedience of the one man the many were made sinners, so also through the obedience of the one man the many will be made righteous' (Romans 5:19 NIV).

'For as in Adam all die, so in Christ all will be made alive' (1 Cor. 15:22 NIV).

The man Adam caused the problem; so the man Jesus solves it. The man Adam passed the problem on to us all; the man Jesus passes on the solution.

Similarly as Eve's action led to the problem, Mary's obedience led to the answer.

So we must understand that the basic differences between men and women were created by God and their different roles were part of his design. The historical events of the Fall determined the rest.

The wonderful counterbalance to all this is that the moment a person believes in the Lord Jesus Christ, whether male of female, they are united by the Holy Spirit with all other believers in the Body of Jesus

1. It was also necessary to bypass the curse on Jeconiah found in Jeremiah 22:30. For a full discussion of this please refer to the tape entitled *The Pedigree of the Messiah* BBS40.

Himself (1 Cor. 12:13). As a result they all become one in Him. So positionally and as far as their salvation is concerned all differences are removed – and not just sex differences. As Galatians explains: 'You are all sons of God through faith in Christ Jesus, for all of you who were baptized into Christ have been clothed with Christ. There is neither Jew nor Greek (racial differences removed), slave nor free (social differences removed), male nor female (sex differences removed), for you are all one in Christ Jesus' (Gal. 3:26-28 NIV).

So female believers as well as male believers are called 'sons' because they are in Jesus who is a son, and as a result they are invested with power and authority and have an inheritance. Equally male believers are members of the Bride of Christ. So, as sons *all* of us are predestined to be adopted.

Before we proceed any further however, we must examine two other aspects of Sonship. The title 'Sons of God' carries with it important implications. Firstly it emphasizes the miraculous work of God in our lives; and secondly it underlines the similarity in nature between ourselves and God. We will examine them in turn.

1. The Sons of God

The phrase 'sons of God' is used of only five people or groups in the Bible and there is a definite link between them. It is used for (i) Adam himself; (ii) Angels; (iii) Israel; (iv) Jesus; and (v) Believers of the Church Age. What is the common link between these? It is that all have resulted through a direct, supernatural, creative act of God Himself and nothing less.

(i) *Adam – 'the Son of God'*

In Luke 3 the genealogy of Mary's line is given and beginning with Jesus it moves back in time through

David and Abraham to Adam himself. Luke 3:38 says 'the son of Enos, the son of Seth, the son of Adam, the Son of God' (NIV). Adam didn't have a mother or father, he was created by God Himself – 'formed' as it says in Genesis 2:7 'from the dust of the ground' (NIV). Hence he bears the title 'Son of God'. His children Cain, Abel, Seth and the 'other sons and daughters' mentioned in Genesis 5:4 (NIV), are never called the sons of God because they are sons of Adam and Eve.

(ii) *Angels – 'Sons of God'.*

Angels are called 'sons of God' several times in the Bible. Job 1:6 tells of a day when the angelic host assembled before the throne of God. Satan, who in Ezekiel 28:14 is himself said to be an angel (a cherub) was among them. The description is significant. 'Now there was a day when the sons of God came to present themselves before the Lord, and Satan also came among them' (NASB).

Later Job confirmed that angels were given this title. In Job 38, 4-7 God spoke to him and said: 'Where were you when I laid the foundation of the earth! Tell me, if you have understanding, who sets its measurements, since you know? Or who stretched the line on it? On what were its bases sunk? Or who laid its corner-stone, when the morning stars sang together, And all the *sons of God* shouted for joy?' (NASB). As this occurred before man's creation it must have reference to angelic beings and not to humans.

Genesis 6 also confirms this when it describes the day when Satan plotted to pollute humankind by infiltrating angelic offspring into the world. 'When men began to increase in number on the earth and daughters were born to them, the sons of God saw that the daughters of men were beautiful, and they married any of them they chose' (Genesis 6:1-2 NIV). As a result of this God's judgment came upon the Earth. Here is the historical event which underlines Greek mythology and it is of great significance that in both Genesis 6 and the Greek tales the mothers are always human and the fathers always heavenly beings. It was a brilliant plan. Satan knew that the Messiah had to be of true human stock, and to stop His coming he sought to destroy true humanity[1].

1 Peter 3:18-20 confirms that the sons of God here are angels. 'For Christ died for sins once for all, the righteous for the unrighteous, to bring you to God. He was put to death in the body but made alive by the Spirit, through whom also he went and preached to *the spirits* in prison who disobeyed long ago when God waited patiently in the days of Noah . . . . ' (NIV).

All this is very interesting, but the significance for us is that angels are called 'sons of God' because they have come from the hand of God Himself and not through any natural process.

Matthew 22:30 confirms this by saying 'At the resurrection people will neither marry nor be given in marriage; they will be like the angels in heaven' (NIV). So angels don't procreate – there aren't any mummy and daddy angels, and no baby angels either! The number is fixed.

(iii) *Israel 'Son of God'.*

We have already quoted Exodus 4: 22-23 where God first described Israel as His Son. The problem for us is that surely the use of the term 'Son of God' in this case breaks the rule because Israel is nothing more than the natural descendants of Abraham, Isaac and Jacob.

On the surface that seems to be the case, but a more detailed study reveals again that without the intervention of God there would have been no Israeli nation. It is not

1. For a detailed description see my book *Victory in Jesus* chapter 3 (Marshalls) and the tape *The Giants of Genesis* STS 89-90.

Abraham, Isaac and Jacob to which our attention must be directed, but to their wives.

The family tree looks quite normal:

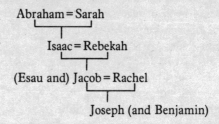

Abraham = Sarah

Isaac = Rebekah

(Esau and) Jacob = Rachel

Joseph (and Benjamin)

What is significant here is that all three men – Abraham, Isaac and Jacob – married women who were unable to have children.

Genesis tells the amazing saga. Abraham and Sarah longed for children, but at the age of 90 Sarah still hadn't conceived. But God had promised. So when Abraham was 99, God appeared and said of Sarah 'As for Sarai your wife, you are no longer to call her Sarai; her name will be Sarah. I will bless her and will surely give you a son by her. I will bless her so that she will be the mother of nations; kings of peoples will come from her' (Genesis 17:15-16 NIV).

We can sympathize with Abraham in his reaction 'Then Abraham fell upon his face, and laughed, and said in his heart, Shall a child be born unto him that is an hundred years old? and shall Sarah, that is ninety years old, bear?' (Gen. 17:17). But it was to be. It was a miracle, a human impossibility made possible by Divine intervention.

But that isn't all, for the same pattern was repeated with Isaac's wife, Rebekah and Jacob's wife Rachel. In every case it was a miracle, and in every case the God of the impossible did the impossible.

So without a direct creative miracle neither Abraham, nor his son nor his grandson would have had offspring.

What does it mean, but that Israel exists because of the creative work of God.

The rule holds.

(iv) *Jesus – 'the Son of God'.*

Jesus is clearly said to be the son of Adam, the son of Abraham, the son of David, the son of Mary, but chiefly the Son of God. The declaration given by the Angel Gabriel to Mary was 'Do not be afraid, Mary, you have found favour with God. You will be with child and give birth to a son, and you are to give him the name Jesus. He will be great and will be called the Son of the Most High' (Luke 1:30-32 NIV).

She queries how this could come to pass – she was a virgin and Joseph an upright man. Gabriel continued 'The Holy Spirit will come upon you, and the power of the Most High will overshadow you. So the holy one to be born will be called the Son of God' (Luke 1:35 NIV).

This was no natural birth. What was impossible to man became glorious reality through the working of God. Let us understand this – a denial of the virgin birth would not only prevent the title 'Son of God' being used of Jesus, but would mean that He was the result of a sinful, illegal sexual act, that he was illegitimate and that His mother was a fornicator. Such thoughts horrify all of us who know the truth. It is not so – His mother was an upright, devoted, pure, young woman and Jesus was the holy child of God's own seed. By a direct act of God, Jesus the Son of God, was born into the world.

(v) *Believers of the Church Age – 'Sons of God'.*

In the New Testament we are clearly declared to be Sons of God. 'You are all sons of God through faith in Christ Jesus' (Gal. 3:26 NIV). We are called by this name because, as we have seen clearly before, our new birth was a miracle of God which was unattainable by any natural act. It was the seed of God coming into us that made us His children, and we are born from above; the heavenly offspring of our heavenly Father.

So here is the rule – the title 'Son of God' is used only of those whose existence depends on God's intervention itself. Certainly, therefore, all believers are sons.

But there is more to Sonship than that – for it actually implies a similarity in nature too.

2. A Similarity of Nature

My interpreter in Sweden is a delightful, talented man called Sven Nyberg. His knowledge of English is excellent and he has been known to enquire about complexities of the language such as the exact difference between 'euphemistic' and 'euphuistic'! Interestingly enough, however, he has also been totally stumped by a word like 'blancmange'. What he and all interpreters find difficult are the idioms which English often uses. 'Tucked up your sleeve'; 'raining cats and dogs'; 'I could eat a horse'; 'to have a bee in one's bonnet' have to be avoided 'like the plague' unless you know that there is a very similar idiom in their language.

In the Greek language there are many idioms too, and its interpreters have similar problems to cope with. But there is no problem in translating the meaning of the English idiom 'he's a chip off the old block'. If the Greeks wanted to show that there was a similarity between and son and his father they simply used the phrase 'he's a son of . . . . ' Unlike the English idiom this was not just restricted to a father-son relationship. The Bible uses it often and in many ways:

'Jesus said unto them, "Can the children (HUIOS) of the bridechamber mourn, as long as the bridegroom is with them"' (Matthew 9:15).

The 'sons of the bridechamber' is an idiom for the guests at the wedding – they are those who are sharing the festive mood and who are as happy and joyful as the bride and groom. If they are mourning they are by definition not 'sons of the bridechamber' because they do not share the feelings of the happy couple.

'And James the son of Zebedee, and John the brother of James; and he surnamed them Boanerges, which is, The sons of thunder.' (Mark 3:17).

The point being made here is that James and John, the children of Zebedee, made a lot of noise and ferment, but most of it was just hot air. Thunder may seem frightening but in fact it results from the rush of air into the vacuum created by the extremely hot fork of electricity. A lot of noise is created but nothing more. So with no ability to put their words into action, they asked Jesus whether they should command fire to fall from heaven to burn up the Samaritans who hadn't received Him (see Luke 9:54) – typical of 'sons of thunder'.

'And Jesus said to them, "The sons (HUIOS) of this age marry and are given in marriage"' (Luke 20:34 NASB).

This implies that the unbeliever has the character and characteristics of the whole world system. 'Chips off the old block'. This is why in Ephesians 2:1 Paul says of us all: 'As for you, you were dead in your transgressions and sins, in which you used to live when you followed the ways of this world and of the ruler of the kingdom of the air, the spirit who is now at work in those who are disobedient. All of us also lived among them at one time, gratifying the cravings of our sinful nature and following its desires and thoughts. Like the rest, we were by nature objects of wrath' (NIV). It was true of us all.

'None of them is lost, but the son of perdition' (John 17:12).

This is a reference to Judas. The word 'PERDITION' is the Greek word 'APOLLUMI' and is translated as 'damnable, or destruction'. This is a picture of his basic character. It is the very character of the devil himself. In Revelation 9:11 it says 'They had as king over them the angel of the Abyss, whose name in Hebrew is Abaddon, and in Greek, Apollyon.' Both names mean 'destroyer'.

It is no surprise, therefore, when we learn that the future character of renown who is called the Man of Sin is also called 'the Son of Perdition'. 2 Thessalonians 2:3 'Let no man deceive you by any means: for that day shall not come, except there come a falling away first, and that man of sin be revealed, the son of perdition.' It is his basic character which is in view.

'And Joses, who by the apostles was surnamed Barnabas, (which is, being interpreted, the son of consolation) a Levite, and of the country of Cyprus having land, sold it, and brought the money, and laid it at the apostles' feet' (Acts 4:36).

Here was a wonderful saint of God whose very life was characterized by consolation and encouragement.

The glory of this is that we are called 'sons of God' and as such we are to be possessors of the character of God Himself. We are like him. In case that seems too generalized the New Testament spells it out for us. In every one of the following Scriptures the phrase 'son of . . . . ' refers to us. We are:

'Sons of your Father'	: (Matt. 5.45 NIV).
'Sons of the bridechamber'	: (Matt. 9:15).
'Sons of the kingdom'	: (Matt. 13:38 NIV).
'Sons of God, being sons of the resurrection'	: (Luke 20:36 NASB)
'Sons of light'	: (John 12:36 NASB)
'Sons of light and sons of day'	: (1 Thess. 5:5 NASB)

We are stamped with the hallmark of God our Father, we have the benefits of the kingdom available to us through the Holy Spirit which is the power 'of the coming age' (Heb. 6:5 NIV), we are joyful people because we have the resurrection power of Jesus in us. Though the world is in darkness we are of the day and are here to 'shine as lights in the world' (Phil. 2:15).

What a privilege it is to be sons of God.

How does God make sure that His resurrection life is seen in us in ever-increasing glory? He trains us as a father trains his own sons.

9

The Preparation of the Sons of God

The process of becoming a son followed a well-mapped route. The child was born into the family and began to receive basic instruction and correction from his parents. As time progressed his attitude and behaviour showed whether he had learned the lessons well and whether he was a responsible person; indeed the parents would often give him tests along the way to see how he was developing. 'He that is faithful in that which is least is faithful also in much' (Luke 16:10). Finally, if the father was satisfied with the boy he would declare him to be his 'Son' and give him the Toga Virilis.

This is the route we would expect God to take with us, but amazingly He has changed the order of things. With us the order is: (a) We are born into His family and begin to grow; (b) early in our lives are declared to be 'sons' and given the Toga Virilis in faith and expectation of full maturity; and *then* (c) we go through the training process to bring us into the experience of Sonship.

The experience of the disciples gives us the pattern. They were born-again and children of God and, as we have seen, they recognized Jesus and were able to 'hear' His words. Once the resurrection had occurred – on the very evening of the resurrection in fact – Jesus appeared to them and said 'Peace be with you! As the Father has sent me, I am sending you.' And with that he breathed on them and said, 'Receive the Holy Spirit' (John 20:21-22 NIV).

Forty days later in Luke 24:49 Jesus then said 'I am going to send you what my Father has promised; but stay in the city until you have been *clothed* with power from on high' (NIV). Sure enough, on the Day of Pentecost the Holy Spirit came down upon them and they were 'clothed' as Jesus had promised.

The word 'clothed' here is very significant for it is a reference to the Toga Virilis – the same garment Jesus received at His adoption. Indeed Luke 4:1 says of Jesus after His baptism that He, 'full of the Holy Spirit, returned from the Jordan and was led by the Spirit in the desert' (NIV). While He received it after 30 years of testing, the disciples received it while they were still raw, immature, unwise and inexperienced people. In fact it was only a matter of days since Peter had denied Jesus three times.

On the Day of Pentecost the disciples, who a month or so before had been a demoralized, disheartened bunch, suddenly came into new authority and spoke with boldness in Jerusalem. It would have been easy for them to think that they had 'arrived' because of this, but in fact it simply marked the beginning of the training period.

When I was first 'endued with power from on high' just a few weeks after my conversion, it was the start of a period of miraculous happenings in my life. Many were converted, many 'filled' with the Holy Spirit, many released from bondages and healed of sicknesses. I, and those in our University group, saw many wonderful things and we seemed to live with a 'pillar of cloud and fire' guiding us every day. The Bible was sparkling with life, and prayer meetings were our delight. Four or five hours of prayer seemed as no time at all.

But after a time things seemed to slow down – miracles

occurred less frequently, prayer became more difficult and the Word of God seemed to be a reservoir which needed pumping, rather than an overflowing fountain. When I first noticed the change I sought God earnestly about it.

He revealed to me my sinfulness – indeed the shambles which was my life – and told me that he had given a foretaste of what was to come. By grace He had allowed us to experience these things, but now would begin a period in which He would begin training us and dealing with our lives. He showed me that so far I had been walking by sight, not by faith. For example, every time I prayed I felt tingling up and down my spine as if the hands of Jesus were touching me. That made me *feel* very close to God, but it wasn't faith but feelings. Soon after He showed me this the tingling stopped. Then it was faith – I had to believe that God was still real and close even though I felt nothing. Just at that time I read Watchman Nee's book *Release of the Spirit* and it confirmed everything the Lord was showing me.

The miracles were generally of the 'still small voice' kind, rather than thunderous, fiery, earth-moving events. For example on May 26th 1969, as I was sitting on a park bench feeling utterly downcast and miserable because of certain areas of sin in my life, I saw a smiling nun walking along the path. I hadn't spoken to a nun before – it wasn't what I considered 'my scene' – but I felt that I just had to talk to her. 'Can you help me?' I said, 'I am a Christian but I feel so low and confused at the moment.' 'My name is Sister Dikla,' she said, 'come with me.' I followed her to a little house just around the corner from where I lived and as we arrived a group of other nuns were arriving too. They were about to have a meeting. They sang and praised for half an hour. They gave me no advice but after the meeting, with a slice of cake in my hand, I learned that they belonged to the Mary sisters of Darmstadt. They gave me Basilea Schlink's book *Those who love Him*. It was God's provision through a miraculous encounter. I never saw them again but I felt as though I had been fed by a God-sent raven.

In Hosea 2:14-15 God described His training programme for Israel: 'I am now going to allure her; I will lead her into the desert and speak tenderly to her. There I will give her back her vineyards, and will make the Valley of Achor a door of hope. There she will sing as in the days of her youth, as in the day she came up out of Egypt' (NIV). The word 'tenderly' here is literally 'to her heart'. That is what was occurring to me during this time. He was showing me my heart. It helped me to know that God was still with me and that He was training me. I knew that He was still there, and that after the desert I would come into my vineyard and 'sing' again as in my youth.

Every miracle now had training associated with it. Before, the miracles had been 'self-contained'; now they had a double edge and achieved something in my personal life. One Sunday morning, for example, as I was walking across the park on my way to church, I saw a foreign girl picking the tulips and daffodils. I couldn't believe my eyes. I decided to stop her and like a good citizen went over and told her that she shouldn't be doing that because then no-one else would be able to enjoy them. Defensively, she turned her back on me. It was clear that she thought I simply wanted them for myself.

So I began to talk to her. She had just arrived in England from Thailand and was on an 'English for Foreign Students' course. She relaxed a little then and decided to walk with me. Her name was Joom (= 'little one') Chumrakrumran. Upon hearing that I was on my way to church, she proudly announced that she was a

Buddhist. 'Jesus good' she said 'but so is Buddha.' Immediately I said 'Jesus is *best*.' I'm not sure whether any evangelistic book on 'How to win Buddhists to Christ' would have said it was the right approach, but it was out of my mouth before I had time to think about it. She was furious and stormed off.

The next morning as the students in our digs sat down for breakfast (congealed scrambled eggs) and began their usual dull conversations – one person was studying advanced mathematics; another physics and another the life of St. Augustine – the door of the dining room opened and in came a new student – Joom Chumrakrumran. She smiled and looked around, but when she saw me her eyes flashed with anger. Throwing her books down, she pointed at me and shouted 'I hate you!' and rushed from the room. I died a thousand deaths in the moments that followed. My fellow-students and my landlady narrowed their eyes, pressed their lips firmly together, raised their eyebrows and gazed knowingly at me. What could I do? I blushed, smiled, nodded and said nothing. My pride was flattened and so was any pretence of being 'normal'.

That evening as I was in my room, there was a knock at my door. It was Joom; tears streaming down her face. As I let her in she began to apologize for the morning's upset. 'I now a Christian' she said. 'What, Joom?' – joy burst into my heart – 'What?' 'Yes' she said. 'I hated you this morning, but when I looked into your eyes I saw Jesus and He loved me. Now I a Christian too.' She was, as well, and became a gleaming light to all the Christians there – a miracle sure enough, but one which cut through the pride and arrogance of my life and exposed it at the same time. He was dealing with me.

I was learning that the *ways* of God, were more important than His acts. 'He made known his ways to Moses, his deeds to the people of Israel' (Psalm 103:7 NIV) and frankly up to this time I'd preferred His acts. How correctly 1John 2:12-14 expresses this.

'I write to you, dear children, because your sins have been forgiven on account of his name. I write to you, fathers, because you have known him who is from the beginning. I write to you, young man, because you have overcome the evil one' (NIV).

This is all of great significance. The children are interested in what they've got and what they've been given; the young men are glorifying in their strength, but the fathers – the mature ones – are thrilled to know God Himself.

Although we may have been given the Toga Virilis and have been empowered from above, let none of us think that means we have *ipso facto* 'made it'. The training is just beginning and it is the Holy Spirit, the One called alongside, who is our Instructor. Jesus said 'But when he, the Spirit of truth, comes, he will guide you into all the truth. He will not speak on his own; he will speak only what he hears, and he will tell you what is yet to come. He will bring glory to me by taking from what is mine and making it known to you' (John 16:13-14 NIV).

Just as the Romans employed Greeks to teach their children, so Jesus has sent the Holy Spirit to lead us into Sonship. In Romans 8:15 He is called 'the spirit of adoption' or as the NIV translates it 'the Spirit of Sonship'.

The Holy Spirit accomplishes three things:

1. He constantly reaffirms to us the fact that we are children of God. 'The Spirit himself testifies with our spirit that we are God's children' (Romans 8:16 NIV).
2. He keeps us ever conscious of the Father. 'You received the Spirit of sonship. And by him we cry, "Abba, Father"' (Romans 8:15 NIV). 'Because you are

sons, God sent the Spirit of his Son into our hearts, the Spirit who calls out, "Abba, Father"' (Gal. 4:6 NIV). Both we and the Holy Spirit cry 'Father.'

3. He matures us until the Family likeness shows. 'But the fruit of the Spirit is love, joy, peace, patience, kindness, goodness, faithfulness, gentleness and self-control' (Gal. 5:22-23 NIV).

A key verse in the maturing process is Romans 8:14. It says 'For as many as are led by the Spirit of God, they are the sons (HUIOS) of God.' In other words, the degree to which an individual is following the Holy Spirit shows how close he is to acting as a son.

We have to ask, what does it mean 'to be led by the Holy Spirit?' The answer is that because the Holy Spirit is Himself God, He is sovereign. That means that He has a definite purpose – the will of God.

We, as believers, have been given the gift of free will, but the mature sons among us are those who have given up their right to do what they want and have decided to do God's will instead. Those who have completely yielded their wills to Him are the sons (HUIOS) of God.

Jesus gives us the perfect example, when in Gethsemane he prays 'Father, if you are willing, take this cup from me; yet not my will, but yours be done' (Luke 22:42 NIV).

In Rome those who received the Toga Virilis were those whose wills totally coincided with their father's will, and so over all matters one will prevailed. The height of maturity is this, that we do exactly what the Father wills. This is true Sonship.

This does not come immediately; we have to learn it. Romans 8 gives us the order in which it is now accomplished:

Romans 8:15 : We receive the Holy Spirit who is 'the Spirit of Sonship' (NIV).

Romans 8:16 : We know that we have joined God's family and are children of God.

Romans 8:17 : Because we are sons, we are also heirs *'if indeed we share in his sufferings that we may also share in his glory.'*

It is this last section which is unpopular today, for most Christians in our welfare state society want things easy. They want to be saved by grace, to live by grace, to be matured by grace and to be rewarded by grace. As a result, they hope they can 'put their feet up and do nothing'. We are certainly saved by grace, but once saved our lives are God's testing grounds in which He deals with us and rewards us according to our deeds.

The results of Sonship come because of our obedience. As we have seen, a child who constantly rebelled and was self-willed just proved he was not of his father's heart, and as a result never came into the benefits and blessings of Sonship. By God's grace we have already been declared 'sons' but, lest there is any misunderstanding about this, let me state categorically that the outworking of it in our lives comes only through our obedience and maturity. The testings and sufferings of our lives are not accidents, but are often the things that God uses to bring us into this maturity. So Paul continues Romans 8 by saying 'I consider that our present sufferings are not worth comparing with the glory that will be revealed in us' (v18 NIV).

If we resist God's training programme, or fight against Him to get our own way, we ourselves will suffer loss and by our actions we will impoverish the believers around us. As someone in the fellowship said recently, 'In God's dealings with our lives, we must be on His side.' How I agree.

It isn't always outright rebellion or resistance on our

part that opposes God's work; it may also be a clever sliding out of the situation. It is not only a thick-shelled nut which is hard to crack, but a slippery one too, for as the pressure is put on, it slips out of the side of the nut-cracker. We must resist this temptation and submit to His dealings.

I remember a meeting several years ago in which a person who had gossiped about me, maligned me and set people against me stood up and made an accusation against me. The accusation was correct—I was guilty of doing what the person said I had done. But, oh, the pressures and mitigating circumstances! As a shocked silence settled on the group, I sat perfectly still. I was being pulled apart inside. One part of me wanted to 'come out fighting' and say 'Yes, I did it, but do you know what I have had to put up with and what has been said about me? I wanted to launch into a tirade and let all my inner hurts come out. The other part of me, however, wanted to go the way of Jesus when He said: 'Blessed are you when people insult you, persecute you and falsely say all kinds of evil against you because of me. Rejoice and be glad . . . . ' (Matt. 5:11-12 NIV), or His later injunction that we should 'resist not evil: but whosoever shall smite thee on thy right cheek, turn to him the other also' (Matt. 5:39). I wanted the first course of action; the Lord wanted the second.

After three or four excruciating minutes I quietly got up from my seat, went over to the person and said 'What you have said is true, I did say it. Please will you forgive me.' It was one of the most cleansing and holy moments of my life.

The Church would be transformed overnight if we all allowed God to have His way, and put the flesh to death. 'Why not rather be wronged? Why not rather be cheated?' (1 Cor. 6:7 NIV). Love 'is not self-seeking, it is not easily angered, it keeps no record of wrongs' (1 Cor. 13:5 NIV).

It is said that a nettle doesn't sting if it is firmly grasped – perhaps it is time we began to use the wrongs, slanders, misunderstandings and other unpleasant things which cross our paths in a positive way. When embraced they might actually not sting. What will be affected is the natural man within us, and the quicker he is put off the better. 'We ourselves, who have the firstfruits of the Spirit, groan inwardly as we wait eagerly for our adoption as sons . . . . ' (Romans 8:23 NIV). All of us who want to press on with God know something of this and it is not helpful when we see others apparently 'free-wheeling' and getting away with it. What a comfort Colossians 1:24 has been to me. 'Now I rejoice in what was suffered for you, and I fill up in my flesh what is still lacking in regard to Christ's afflictions, for the sake of His Body which is the Church' (NIV). If this is what the Lord requires, then so be it – and what a privilege that we should be allowed to achieve something eternal through our ephemeral lives.

The Holy Spirit acts in our lives on behalf of our Father in heaven, and He teaches, rebukes and corrects us to train us in righteousness. We must now resist or refuse His correction.

Hebrews 12:5-12 deals very specifically with our Father's discipline. 'And you have forgotten the word of encouragement that addresses you as sons (HUIOS): "My son, do not make light of the Lord's discipline, and do not lose heart when he rebukes you because the Lord disciplines those whom he loves, and he punishes everyone he accepts as a son." Endure hardship as discipline; God is treating you as sons. For what son is not disciplined (and everyone undergoes discipline), then you are illegitimate children and not true sons. Moreover, we have all had human fathers who disciplined us and we respected them for it. How much more should we submit to the Father of our spirits and live! Our fathers disciplined us for a little while as they thought best; but God disciplines us for our good, that we may share in his holiness. No discipline seems pleasant at the time, but painful. Later on, however, it produces a harvest of righteousness and peace for those who have been trained by it. Therefore, strengthen your feeble arms and weak knees!' (NIV).

The whole passage deals with the discipline of God which leads us to mature Sonship. We must not be surprised when these things occur. Of course, there is a natural desire in all of us to be treated as babies (see chapter 5), but just as our children receive a shock as we begin to expect self-discipline and order from them (helping with the washing-up; clearing away their toys etc.) so the day soon comes when we find God disciplining us. If we do not submit to it, or if in some way we show ourselves unwilling to be trained by God, then the discipline will intensify. The easiest way is the path of submission to God. Rebellious children never prosper in the long run.

Certainly if we refuse to accept our Father's training we will never see the full effects of Sonship in our lives. He desires maturity from us and He will do whatever is necessary to achieve the holiness, sanctification and obedience that is entailed. Our wills must be given over to His will.

In the days of the knights of England, the term 'yield' meant 'to give up'. The sword point was at your throat and it was your only choice. God wants us to yield to Him voluntarily. 'Yield yourselves unto God, as those that are alive from the dead, and your members as instruments of righteousness unto God' (Romans 6:13).

If we can clearly see the aim of God's discipline – to bring us to the place where our lives show forth the effects of being Sons – it will help us to understand the things that come into our lives. There is a purpose to it all – something wonderful, hinted at by Paul when in his letter to Timothy he mysteriously says 'If we suffer, we shall also reign with him' (2 Tim. 2:12). The full glory of Sonship is something which awaits us all, and for eternity we will enjoy its fruits.

10

If Sons, Then Heirs

The envelopes lay with the others on the doormat. Big, thick, brown envelopes usually mean work—a form to fill in, a testimonial to write or some manuscript to check—and therefore it was the last I opened. The letter began 'Please find enclosed a copy of the Will of Miss B. M. Glencross . . . . ' I sat down.

'Glen', as we all affectionately called her, had become a Christian late in life, just three or four years earlier. She had announced to a surprised community that she was retiring and, therefore, closing the private school she had run for many years. Two members of the Fellowship here had in years past sent their children to her school and so took the opportunity to invite her over for supper. During the evening they described what the Lord had done for them and they invited Glen along to the Fellowship. She sat apparently unmoved through her first meeting—a small, thin lady with short white hair—and it looked every bit as if she were there under pressure. In fact, however, it was to be the first of many meetings for her and she soon surrendered her life to Christ.

What wonderful things God did for her too! After a year I received a letter from her: 'What joy and peace I feel, I can hardly believe God has done all this for me.' The doctors had actually given her only six months to live, but the Lord in His grace gave her three more years.

She was a living testimony to answered prayer.

Just before she died she asked me to take her funeral and said to me 'Really let them know, Roger; they need to hear the truth.' I had told her that I never ask for a fee when I take a funeral, but after the service her solicitor (under strict instructions from her) handed me an envelope with a cheque for £20 in it. I thought no more of her estate, assuming that she would do what she had said she would three years previously, and leave it all to the various animal charities she supported.

In the last year of her life, however, she had changed her will. Having had so little time to work for God here on Earth she had been determined to go out with a bang! and so had left half of her substantial estate to the Fellowship here, and half to the London Healing Mission.

I can remember the sheer joy which overwhelmed my being as I read the letter, and the cries of joy which echoed down the phone as I shared the news with others. We had never had anything like it before.

There is a day coming, however, in which all of us who are God's children will receive an inheritance, and by all accounts it will be such a glorious and exciting day that what happened to our Fellowship through 'Glen', will pale into insignificance in comparison. The Bible promises every one of us 'an inheritance that can never perish, spoil or fade – kept in heaven for you, who through faith are shielded by God's power until the coming of the salvation that is ready to be revealed in the last time' (1 Peter 1:4-5 NIV).

We have already seen that this inheritance is an essential aspect of Sonship for it is only the Sons who receive it. In the book of Galatians, however, Paul adds a warning. 'What I am saying is that as long as the heir is a child, he is no different from a slave, although he owns the whole estate. He is subject to guardians and trustees until the time set by his father. So also, when we were children, we were in slavery under the basic principles of the world. But when the time had fully come, God sent his Son, born of a woman, born under law, to redeem those under law, that we might receive the full rights of sons. Because you are sons, God sent the Spirit of his Son into our hearts, the Spirit who calls out, "Abba, Father." So you are no longer a slave, but a son; and since you are a son, God has made you also an heir' (Gal. 4:1-7 NIV).

The truth of this is very obvious, and yet very profound. An immature child may officially be heir to the whole estate, but while he is immature he is under the authority of others and is therefore no better off than anyone else. It is only when he comes to full maturity that the legal position becomes a reality in his life and he finds the fulness of the inheritance at his disposal. In our lives it is the completed work of Jesus which allows us to come into full maturity and which, therefore, enables us to partake of the inheritance.

A few years ago the Lord revealed to me that our inheritance came in three parts which were pictured by the contents of the Ark of the Covenant. The Ark itself was a rectangular box, two cubits long, one cubit wide and one and a half cubits high. It was made of wood overlaid with gold, and Moses was instructed to put it into the Most Holy Place or Holy of Holies in the Tabernacle.

The writer to the Hebrews describes this in Hebrews 9:3-4. 'Behind the second curtain was a room called the Most Holy Place, in which resided the golden altar of incense and the gold-covered ark of the covenant. This ark contained the golden jar of manna, Aaron's rod that had budded, and the stone tablets of the covenant' (NIV).

We don't know when Aaron's rod and the jar of manna were removed from the Ark, but by the time of Solomon only the stone tablets were left (1 Kings 8:9). Here, however, we are concerned with all three. Usually commentators have said that they represent either God's provision for Man, or the way in which man has sinned.

	MAN'S SIN	GOD'S PROVISION
STONE TABLETS	Man has broken God's Law	The Law for Man's moral needs
GOLDEN JAR OF MANNA	Man has rejected God's provision	Food for Man's physical needs
AARON'S ROD	Man has rebelled against God's authority	Authority for Man's spiritual needs

But God, who turns cursing into blessing, has also chosen that these three things should represent the fulness which is our inheritance. We will see them in turn.

The Stone Tablets

When two neighbouring countries entered into a covenant with one another in the Ancient World, two complete copies of the covenant were made, and were placed on either side of the common border. Following this pattern God wrote two complete copies of His Law[2] and put them both in the place where God and Man would meet – their common border – in the Tabernacle.

For us these tablets represent the fact that God's law will be perfectly fulfilled in us. The terms of any covenant were that if one or other party kept the agreement perfectly, many

---

1. See John Phillips *Exploring Hebrews* Moody Press.
2. The idea that five commandments were on one stone and five on the other is wrong.

blessings would be theirs, but if they broke it, cursing would just as surely follow.

Fallen Man breaks God's law constantly, but the promise for us is that His Law will be perfected in us forever, and therefore, that all the blessings interwoven in the Law will be ours. Just as sons received part of their inheritance at their adoption, we receive something of ours in this life. Jesus kept God's law perfectly while He was on the Earth and through the Holy Spirit the blessings He released by His obedience have in some measure become ours. 'For what the law was powerless to do in that it was weakened by the sinful nature, God did by sending his own Son in the likeness of sinful man, in order *that the righteous requirements of the law might be fully met in us*, who do not live according to the sinful nature but according to the Spirit' (Romans 8:3-4 NIV).

It is in eternity, however, that we will come into the full blessings of God. 'For this reason Christ is the mediator of a new covenant, that those who are called may receive the promised eternal inheritance – now that he has died as a ransom to set them free from the sins committed under the first covenant' (Heb. 9:15).

The Golden Pot of Manna

In Revelation 2:17 believers are given a promise. 'He who has an ear, let him hear what the Spirit says to the churches. To him who overcomes,[1] I will give some of the *hidden manna*.'

The only other hidden manna we have reference to in the Bible is that hidden from sight in the Ark of the Covenant. Manna represented God's total provision i.e. all that Man would need for ever and ever.

1. A title for all born-again believers. See *Victory in Jesus* pages 124-126.

124

The power that is within us is the power of eternal life and we have an everlasting, glorious resurrection body which will be exactly like the resurrection body of Jesus. Speaking of the resurrection, Paul describes Christ as 'the firstfruits' (1 Cor. 15:23 NIV). The firstfruit on a tree shows what the rest of the harvest will be like and so 'we know that when he appears, we shall be like him . . . . (1 John 3:2 NIV).

Our resurrection bodies, which are part of our inheritance, will never grow faint or weary; while we *can* eat there will be no need to because our bodies will not grow hungry or thirsty. They will never age nor become ill because the power within us, the hidden manna, will be enough to sustain us for ever.

This is the reason why the Bible suggests that our resurrected bodies will have no blood in them. Luke 24, 39 is phrased very specifically. Jesus appeared to the startled disciples in His resurrection body and 'He said to them "Why are you troubled, and why do doubts rise in your minds? Look at my hands and my feet. It is I myself! Touch me and see; a ghost does not have flesh and bones, as you see I have"' (NIV). The phrase 'flesh and bones' is an unusual one. In both English and Greek the normal expression would be 'flesh and blood', but here it is scrupulously avoided. Could it be that it is a deliberate omission to show the absence of blood?

Medically, blood would be unnecessary for the resurrection body. Blood acts as a link between our bodies and the world around us, taking in everything we need from the environment. For example, the oxygen from the atmosphere is mixed with blood in the lungs and is then transported all around our bodies in the blood stream. The waste carbon dioxide is then returned to the blood and finally exhaled back into the atmosphere.

Similarly, food is taken in through the mouth, digested

by the stomach and bowels, and the nutrients are spread throughout the body by the blood. It is the channel through which the body receives what it needs from the world.

The resurrection body, however, has no such need – God's provision for it is enough for it to be independent from its surroundings. So the blood supply will be unnecessary. The hidden manna is the power of an endless life and the resurrection body is the mansion Jesus is preparing for us (John 14:2 and 2 Cor. 5:1-5).

The Rod of Aaron

In terms of inheritance the rod of Aaron represents the authority which we are going to receive for eternity. Moses was faced with continual criticism and insurrection and the Lord told him to take twelve staffs, each one inscribed with the name of the leader of one of the tribes. The staff for the tribe of Levi was to have Aaron's name on it. They were left overnight in the Tabernacle, and in the morning the staff with Levi's name on it 'had budded and blossomed and produced almonds' (Num. 17:8 NIV). This showed that Aaron was the one God had chosen to have authority.

Unlike our eternal perfection and our resurrection bodies, which we all receive equally, the authority we inherit will vary and with it we will be rewarded for the lives we have lived here on the Earth.

Jesus made this very clear in His teaching. 'Anyone who receives a prophet because he is a prophet *will receive a prophet's reward*, and anyone who receives a righteous man because he is a righteous man *will receive a righteous man's reward*. And if anyone gives a cup of cold water to one of these little ones because he is my disciple, I tell you the truth, he *will certainly not lose his reward*' (Matt. 10:41-42 NIV). 'Blessed are you when

126

men hate you when they exclude you and insult you and reject your name as evil, because of the Son of Man. Rejoice in that day and leap for joy, because *great is your reward in heaven*' (Luke 6:22-23 NIV).

But love your enemies, do good to them, and lend to them without expecting to get anything back. Then *your reward will be great . . . .* ' (Luke 6:35 NIV).

The reward which is primarily for the future varies according to the degree to which His words have been obeyed.

'Then Jesus said to his disciples, "If anyone would come after me, he must deny himself and take up his cross and follow me. For whoever wants to save his life will lose it, but whoever loses his life for me will find it. What good will it be for a man if he gains the whole world, yet forfeits his soul? Or what can a man give in exchange for his soul? *For the Son of Man is going to come in his Father's glory with his angels, and then he will reward each person according to what he has done*' (Matt. 16:24-27 NIV).

This reward is not automatic but depends on how we have used what God has given us: whether we have lived by the Spirit, and whether we have lived for God's Kingdom or the world. The parable of the talents covers the rewards given for faithfulness and true productivity, and in it we see the principles at work. A wealthy man about to embark on a lengthy journey decided to give a capital sum to three of his servants. One received five talents, another two talents and the third one talent. A 'talent' was a weight of gold generally reckoned to be worth 20 years' salary, and so the amount of money given to each was substantial – 100 years' salary; 40 years' salary and 20 years' salary respectively.

The servants were to use the money in any way they wanted with the object of increasing it, and two of the three succeeded in their task by the time the owner returned. The one with five talents had increased it to ten; the one with two to four. However, the person with only one talent hadn't increased it at all, and as a result he was castigated most severely and removed (see Matt. 25:14-30 NIV).

The lessons we learn from this parable are very important. We have first to realize that everything we have has been given to us by God Himself. He is the One of whom David said 'The earth is the Lord's, and everything in it, the world, and all who live in it' (Psalm 24:1 NIV). Whatever we possess is not truly ours, but just on loan for a short time from God. That includes health, good looks, intelligence, strength and anything else. It is tragic that people in the world have regarded these things as their own and squander them on personal pleasures. I shudder to think that, when on that coming day they have to give an account of how they have used those talents they will have nothing to report. Hopefully those of us who are believers will live our lives in the knowledge that we will one day give an account before God and conduct ourselves more wisely.

It is very important for us to realize from the parable of the talents tht the servant who was given five talents and he who was given two receive equal reward. In both cases the initial investment was doubled and both are commended with the same words. Verses 21 and 23 of Matthew 25 are identical: 'Well done, good and faithful servant! You have been faithful with a few things; I will put you in charge of many things. Come and share your master's happiness!' (NIV).

Here is true equality. No matter how much or how little a person has, his reward is given on the basis of increase and *not* on his total assets. An example will explain this.

If one person, Mr A., has 1000 chances to serve the

Lord and uses 500 of them, then his success rate is 1 in 2. Another person, Mr B., may have many fewer chances, say only 100, but if he makes use of just 50 of these, he also has a success rate of 1 in 2. The reward for both will therefore be equal.

The quality of our work is also judged – whether in the flesh, or as in Jesus' case, by the power of God. Paul describes how the judgment of our works is carried out.

'For no-one can lay any foundation other than the one already laid, which is Jesus Christ. If any man builds on his foundation using gold, silver, costly stones, wood, hay or straw, his work will be shown for what it is, because the Day will bring it to light. It will be revealed with fire, and the fire will test the quality of each man's work. If what he has built survives, he will receive his reward' (1 Cor. 3:11-17 NIV).

Giving and fasting are two of the examples of such work found in the New Testament.

'"Be careful not to do your 'acts of righteousness' before men, to be seen by them. If you do, you will have no reward from your Father in heaven. So when you give to the needy, do not announce it with trumpets, as the hypocrites do in the synagogue and on the streets, to be honoured by men. I tell you the truth, *they have received their reward in full*. But when you give to the needy, do not let your left hand know what your right hand is doing, so that your giving may be in secret. Then your Father, who sees what is done in secret, will reward you"' (Matt. 6:1-4 NIV).

'"When you fast, do not look sombre as the hypocrites do, for they disfigure their faces to show men they are fasting. I tell you the truth, *they have received their reward in full*. But when you fast, put oil on your head and wash your face, so that it will not be obvious to men that you are fasting, but only to your Father, who is unseen; and

129

your Father, who sees what is done in secret, will reward you'" (Matt. 6:16-18 NIV).

The works of the flesh will be burned up; those achieved in the Spirit will remain and we will be rewarded accordingly.

Our reward comes in the form of crowns – the symbol of authority – which God Himself will give us. There are two words for crown used in the Bible – DIADEMA and STEPHANOS.

Diadema

A diadema was a blue ribbon which the Persian kings tied around their turbans. The more countries they ruled, the more blue ribbons they would have. Jesus at the Second Advent is described as having 'many crowns' (diadema) on His head (Rev. 19:12), for He is the King of the whole Earth. Because all believers have been made kings, all of us will have at least one.

Stephanos

This was a crown given to someone for an achievement. Every person who won a race or any competition was given one. These are the crowns we receive as our reward; they are not given automatically.

1. *A Crown of Righteousness*

Given to those who have 'fought the good fight' and who have stayed true to God's purpose in their lives (2 Tim. 4:7-8 NIV).

2. *An Incorruptible Crown*

For the spiritual athletes (1 Cor. 9:25-27).

3. *A Crown of Life*

For those who, despite opposition, persecution and even torture and death remain faithful (Rev. 2:10 and James 1:12).

4. *A Crown of Rejoicing*

For the believers who have selflessly laid down their lives for the work (1 Thess. 2:19).

5. *A Crown of Glory*

For elders who have ruled well and been faithful (1 Peter 5:3-4).

Some may ask 'Well, won't that mean that for all eternity some will live in regret, and be constantly reminded of their lack of success as they see others with more crowns?' The answer to this is 'no' for two reasons.

First of all everyone will be completely happy and satisfied. A person with a large appetite is 100% satisfied when given a large meal. A person with a small appetite is also 100% satisfied when given a small meal. Both are completely happy even though treated differently. Heaven will have none who are disappointed or discontent.

Secondly – and most wonderful of all – when we receive our crowns we throw them at the feet of Jesus Himself. This is the truth revealed in Revelation 4: 10-11, 'The four and twenty elders shall fall down before him that sat on the throne, and worship him that liveth for ever and ever, and cast their crowns before the throne, saying: "Thou art worthy, O lord, to receive glory and honour and power: for thou hast created all things, and for thy pleasure they are and were created"'. Jesus receives all the glory.

Here is our full inheritance – the fulness of blessing, a resurrection body and a position of authority.

In view of all these things we should take care how we live out our lives: indeed Paul tells us to work out our 'salvation with fear and trembling' (Phil. 2:12). The people of the world, whose minds are darkened, think that they can carry on living without giving an account to anyone, but they are people of the night and will one day wake up to find that they have deceived themselves.

But we are people of the day, and we know the truth. What lives ought we to live then? If there is no judgment, then as Paul says, everyone should 'eat and drink, for tomorrow we die' (1 Cor. 15:32 NIV). It is sheer foolishness to live otherwise and certainly people who try to live godly lives 'are to be pitied more than all men' (1 Cor. 15:19 NIV). But we *know* that a judgment is coming, and in the light of that we are the wise men. What does it matter if we are despised and rejected by the world or if we suffer the loss of all things? It makes perfect sense in eternity.

Jim Eliot expressed it perfectly: 'He is no fool who gives what he cannot keep to gain that which he cannot lose.' God who sees in secret *will* reward openly. That judgment day puts sense and reason into all that happens to us and makes it clear. Indeed it is the worldly people who live constantly for this world's goods and for status who are the pitiable ones. 'They think it strange that you do not plunge with them into the same flood of dissipation, and they heap abuse on you. But they will have to give account to him who is ready to judge the living and the dead' (1 Peter 4:4-5 NIV). If we were to keep this constantly in mind, it would transform our lives.

Finally, let us remember that both Esau and Reuben lost their birthrights and their inheritance because of instability and lack of self-control. Their deeds are recorded in order that we should not repeat their mistakes.

God requires of us that we act like the mature Sons we are, in the full and firm knowledge that God will one day say 'Well done, good and faithful servant! . . . . Come and share your master's happiness!' (Matt. 25:21 NIV).

What greater incentive could there be for us to be whole-hearted in all we do. 'Whatever you do, work at it with all your heart, as working for the Lord, not for men, since you know that you will receive an inheritance from the Lord as a reward' (Col. 3:23-24 NIV).

11

The Royal Family

There are times in my reading of the Bible when I wish God had allowed us a little insight into the reaction of people involved in the events. What was the scene like, for example, when Rahab and her family emerged from her house on the wall and realized that all the rest of the wall had collapsed, leaving her little section standing alone? Were there tears or laughter? Did they join hands and dance? Did all the people gather round to see the one upright pinnacle and its red cord still dangling from the window?

Or what exactly happened after the workers on the tower of Babel realized that their neighbours had developed new languages? I long for a full description of the scene of chaos and the gradual relief as groups of people who could still understand one another formed.

In the life of Jesus there is one incident about which no comment is made but which I am sure must have generated great excitement. It is found in the 17th chapter of Matthew's Gospel. 'After Jesus and his disciples arrived in Capernaum, the collectors of the two-drachma tax came to Peter and asked, "Doesn't your teacher pay the temple tax?" "Yes, he does," he replied. When Peter came into the house, Jesus was the first to speak. "What do you think, Simon?" He asked. "From whom do the kings of the earth collect duty and taxes —

from their own sons or from others?" "From others," Peter answered. "Then the sons are exempt," Jesus said to him. "But so that we may not offend them, go to the lake and throw out your line. Take the first fish you catch; open its mouth and you will find a four drachma coin. Take it and give it to them for my tax and yours'" (v24-27 NIV).

I would love to have seen Peter's face. The tax referred to in this incident was not a Roman tax but one which God demanded in the law. Every Israelite of twenty years of age and over paid it. Exodus 30:12 says 'When you take a census of the Israelites to count them, each one must pay the Lord a ransom for his life at the time he is counted' (NIV). The money was given to God and was used for the upkeep of the Temple.

It was obvious, therefore, that Jesus and the disciples would be asked to pay it along with everyone else. Jesus, however, knew that he could legitimately miss it. His Father in heaven was the King of the whole Earth. 'For God is the King of all the earth; sing to him a psalm of praise. God reigns over the nations; God is seated on his holy throne' (Psalm 47:7-8 NIV), and because kings do not exact tax from their own sons God would not expect Him pay.

Obviously the people wouldn't have understood this, and so Jesus performed a miracle so that they wouldn't be offended. He told Peter to go fishing and to look in the mouth of the first fish he caught. Inside its mouth, as Jesus had said, Peter found the money for the tax.

I wonder whether Peter realized the real lesson that Jesus was teaching. By this time Peter knew that Jesus was God's son, the Son of the King of Kings, and therefore, a king Himself but did he spot the implications for himself? While the tax demanded was a two-drachma tax, it was a four drachma coin which Peter found in the fish's mouth. As Jesus explained 'for my tax and yours' (v27 NIV).

What Jesus was declaring was that not only was *He* the King's son and part of the Royal Family, but Peter, and therefore the rest of the disciples, were too! Those who had been born of poor Galilean stock through the natural birth, and who were largely unlearned and untaught, had been born again into the Royal Family of God. This was not the so-called royalty of a banana republic or Balkan state, but a royalty which far exceeded that of the House of Windsor. It was the most royal and exalted household that will ever exist – the Royal Household of God.

It didn't only apply to the disciples, either. Every member of the Church of Jesus Christ is part of the same Royal Family. Speaking of members of the Church, Peter says 'But you are a chosen people, *a royal priesthood*, a holy nation, a people belonging to God, that you may declare the praises of him who called you out of darkness into his wonderful light. Once you were not a people, but now you are the people of God' (1 Peter 2:9-10 NIV). John confirms this in Revelation 1:5-6 'Unto him that loved us, and washed us from our sins in his own blood, and hath made us kings and priests unto God and his Father.'

Here again the limitations of the natural birth are totally overcome through the new birth. In the Old Testament only those born into the tribe of Judah could be of royal birth, and only those from Levi could be priests. We, however, whether Jew or Gentile, can be both royal and priestly without any such restriction. *That* which is impossible in the flesh is gloriously possible in the spirit, for our Father in heaven is King over a whole family of kings.

Unlike our royal families who have an extensive history but no certainty of the future, we have a very short past history (born to our Father in heaven) but a very wonderful and clearly laid out future. As we have seen, our future inheritance includes the comprehensive blessings of a fulfilled covenant, a resurrection body with the power of endless life, and varying degrees of authority. For all eternity we are going to reign as kings with Jesus.

Before the call of Abraham the first born son was a very significant person. He received three things in his inheritance:

1. The rulership.
2. The priesthood.
3. A double portion of inheritance.

If the family was small and insignificant these operated on a small scale. If, however, it was the chief family of the land he would be King, High Priest and a very wealthy man. Melchizedek, for example, is described in Genesis 14:18 as 'king of Salem . . . priest of God Most High'. This was the normal rule of inheritance in the Middle East. It was the rule which applied in Israel too until Jacob's sons' days. Of Jacob's sons, Reuben, the first born, was due to inherit all three of these. Unfortunately he was a very unstable individual indeed and because of his instability, like Esau before him, he lost that to which he was entitled. This weakness led him to have sexual relations with Jacob's concubine Bilhah (Gen. 35:22), which was greatly offensive to his father.

Jacob on his death-bed said to him: 'Reuben, thou art my firstborn, my might, and the beginning of my strength, the excellency of dignity and the excellency of power: *unstable as water*, thou shalt not excel; because thou wentest up to thy father's bed; then defiledst thou it; he went up to my couch' (Gen. 49:3-4). The result of this was that the benefits which were normally his went to his brethren.

1 Chronicles 5:1 says of Reuben that 'he was the first

born, but when he defiled his father's marriage bed, his rights as first born were given to the sons of Joseph son of Israel; so he could not be listed in the genealogical record in accordance with his birthright, and though Judah was the strongest of his brothers and a ruler came from him, the rights of the first born belonged to Joseph' (NIV). The fact is that Reuben lost the rulership to Judah; the priesthood to Levi and the double-portion to Joseph (who had two sons Ephraim and Manasseh, who both received a full portion).

Jesus is of the tribe of Judah and, as proved by the detailed genealogies to the Gospels of Matthew and Luke, He is the King of Israel. But of more significance to us than this is that Jesus has again restored the birthright of the first born. Hebrews says of Jesus 'But God said to him, "You are my Son: today I have become your Father." And he says in another place, "You are a priest for ever, *in the order of Melchizedek*"' (Heb. 5:5-6 NIV). Jesus is the first born in many respects:

1. 'The first born among many brothers' (Romans 8:29 NIV).
2 . 'The First born over all creation' (Col. 1:15 NIV).
3 . 'The first born from among the dead' (Col 1: 18 NIV).

As such He can claim rulership, priesthood and the double-portion.

He is King over the whole creation; King of the living and of the dead. He is the Head of the Church; 'And God placed all things under his feet and appointed him to be head over everything for the church, which is his body, the fulness of him who fills everything in every way' (Eph 1:22-23 NIV).

He is the Great High Priest for the whole of creation.

138

'Salvation is found in no-one else, for there is no other name under heaven given to men by which we must be saved.' (Acts 4:12 NIV). Reject His Mediatorship and there is no other help available.

He also inherits all things. He inherits believers: 'his glorious inheritance in the saints' (Eph 1:18 NIV); or as the Psalmist said 'Blessed is the nation whose God is the Lord, the people he chose for his inheritance' (Psalm 33:12 NIV). He also inherits the whole earth: 'Rise up, O God, judge the earth, for all the nations are your inheritance' (Psalm 82:8 NIV).

These are the rights of the first-born and Jesus receives all of them.

The day is coming when Jesus will return to the Earth in power and great glory, and on that day the kingdoms of this world will become the kingdom of our God. On that day every knee shall bow, 'in heaven and on earth and under the earth, and every tongue confess that Jesus Christ is Lord' (Phil 2:10-11 NIV). This is the inheritance of Jesus, 'For by him all things were created: things in heaven and on earth, visible and invisible, whether thrones or powers or rulers of authorities . . . .' (Col. 1:16 NIV). Not only will human governments be overthrown and upturned, but the angelic council which has attempted to direct the world's affairs will also be overthrown. Hebrews 2:5 tell us that 'It is not to angels that he has subjected the world to come' (NIV). 'The Lord will punish the powers in the heavens above and the kings on the earth below' (Isaiah 24:21 NIV).

A new era begins with the triumphal return of Jesus. He does not come alone! As Enoch declared of old "Behold, the Lord cometh with ten thousands of his saints, to execute judgment upon all . . . . " (Jude 14 and 15). The Church of the first born, we who believe in the Lord Jesus Christ, return with Him. While the Earth has undergone the plagues of the Tribulation, the Bride of Jesus, the Church, has been with Him in heaven being prepared for her future role. The Second Advent marks the intervention of the King and His family into history again.

'I saw heaven standing open and there before me was a white horse, whose rider is called Faithful and True. With justice he judges and makes war. His eyes are like blazing fire, and on his head are many crowns. He has a name written on him that no-one but he himself knows. He is dressed in a robe dipped in blood, and his name is the Word of God. The armies of heaven were following him, riding on white horses and dressed in fine linen, white and clean' (Rev. 19:11-14 NIV).

From that day on we, the Royal Family of God, rule with Him and come into our inheritance. The promises about this are many and varied:

Our Rulership

'To him who overcomes, I will give the right to sit with me on my throne, just as I overcame and sat down with my Father on his throne' (Rev 3:21 NIV).

'And hast made us unto our God kings and priests: and *we shall reign* on the earth' (Rev. 5:10).

In the Gospels Jesus confirms it:

'And I confer on you a kingdom, just as my Father conferred one on me, so that you may eat and drink at my table in my kingdom and sit on thrones, judging the twelve tribes of Israel' (Luke 22:29-30 NIV).

'Jesus said to them "I tell you the truth, at the renewal of all things, when the Son of Man sits on his glorious throne, you who have followed me will also sit on twelve thrones, judging the twelve tribes of Israel. And everyone who has left houses or brothers or sisters or father or mother or children or fields for my sake will receive a hundred times as much and will inherit eternal life. But many who are first will be last, and many who are last will be first' (Matt. 19:28-30 NIV).

Paul confirmed it, too:

'Do you not know that the saints will judge the world?' (1 Cor. 6:2 NIV).

'Do you not know that we will judge angels?' (1 Cor 6:3 NIV).

Our Inheritance

'Blessed are the meek, for they will inherit the earth' (Matt. 5:5 NIV).

'Come, you who are blessed by my Father; take your inheritance, the kingdom prepared for you since the creation of the world' (Matt. 25:34 NIV).

'Then the sovereignty, power and greatness of the kingdoms under the whole heaven will be handed over to the saints, the people of the Most High' (Daniel 7:27 NIV).

After Jesus returns He will establish His throne in Jerusalem and from Jerusalem He Himself will reign and we with Him. Our jurisdiction will be over both the heavens and the earth. As we will have our resurrection bodies we will be unconstrained and able without effort to discharge our duties. This at last is the fulfilment of Romans 8:23, for at this time we receive 'our adoption as sons, the redemption of our bodies' (NIV). Because we are released and have the fulness of the 'glorious freedom of the children of God' (Romans 8:21 NIV), the creation itself will also be released.

In that period of history Satan and all his angels are bound; the ungodly are removed and the curse on Creation which came in with Adam is annulled. What a glorious earth is presented to us in the pages of Scripture. Deserts bloom, rain falls in abundance and every field brings forth a full harvest. 'The desert and the parched land will be glad;

the wilderness will rejoice and blossom . . . . Water will gush forth in the wilderness and streams in the desert' (Isaiah 35:1 and 6 NIV).

I remember standing by Ennerdale Lake in Cumbria on a fine June afternoon and seeing the greens and blues; I thought it was like Paradise. The Spirit of the Lord spoke to me and said that under Jesus' reign I would see beauty the like of which I have never beheld. Animals will lose all fear and ferocity. 'The wolf will live with the lamb, the leopard will lie down with the goat, the calf and the lion and the yearling together; and a little child will lead them. The cow will feed with the bear, their young will lie down together, and the lion will eat straw like the ox. The infant will play near the hole of the cobra, and the young child put his hand into the viper's nest' (Isaiah 11:6-8 NIV).

There will be universal peace and prosperity within a perfect environment. Above all God's Word will be universally taught: 'They will neither harm nor destroy on all my holy mountain, for the earth will be full of the knowledge of the LORD as the waters cover the sea' (Isaiah 11:9 NIV).

What a day it will be. Yet wonder of all wonders, the creation will only be reflecting the glory which we the Sons of God will have on that day. It is the day of the Revealed Sons of Glory. Fullness of blessing under God's universal provision and authority will be our inheritance. But the Church will not be alone in its blessing. All Old Testament and Tribulational saints will be raised – Job will see God, as he knew he would. He expressed his faith powerfully in Job 19:25-27 'I know that my Redeemer lives and that in the end he will stand upon the earth. And after my skin has been destroyed, yet in my flesh I will see God; I myself will see him with my own eyes – I, and not another' (NIV).

On the Earth Israel will be chief among the nations and will know the full blessing of God's covenant with them. God will fulfil the words of Amos 9:13-15: '"The days are coming," declares the lord, "when the reaper will be overtaken by the ploughman and the planter by the one treading grapes. New wine will drip from the mountains and flow from all the hills. I will bring back my exiled people Israel; they will rebuild the ruined cities and live in them. They will plant vineyards and drink their wine; they will make gardens and eat their fruit. I will plant Israel in their own land never again to be uprooted from the land I have given them," says the Lord your God' (NIV).

'The nation of kingdom that will not serve you will perish; it will be utterly ruined' (Isaiah 60:12 NIV).

Initially our rulership will be confined to this present earth and will last for the 1000 years of Christ's reign. 'I saw thrones on which were seated those who had been given authority to judge' (Rev 20:4 NIV). We will share this place with those believers who have been martyred in the Tribulation. 'And I saw the souls of those who had been beheaded because of their testimony for Jesus and because of the word of God . . . . They came to life and reigned with Christ a thousand years . . . . Blessed and holy are those who have part in the first resurrection. The second death has no power over them, but they will be priests of God and of Christ and will reign with him for a thousand years' (Rev. 20: 4 and 6 NIV).

After the rebellion which follows the 1000 years of Christ's reign on the Earth, the old heaven and earth are removed and there is at last the establishment of 'a new heaven and a new earth' (Rev. 21:1 NIV).

The Royal Family continue to reign and they do so forever and ever. 'The throne of God and of the Lamb will be in the city, and his servants will serve him. They will see his face, and his name will be on their foreheads. There will be no more night. They will not need the light of a lamp or the light of the sun, for the Lord God will give them light. And they will reign for ever and ever' (Rev. 22:3-5 NIV).

God has planned all of this for His wonderful family. 'How great is the love the Father has lavished on us that we should be called children of God!' (1 John 3:1 NIV).

Here is our ceiling, our vocation – we need to keep it in mind as we walk on this Earth. If we know we are going on a journey we make careful preparations in advance. How much more surely must we prepare ourselves for the day of our authority, which is coming as surely as day follows night.

It is no use thinking we can be royalty in name only, we must also act like royalty.

The story is told that when our present Queen, Elizabeth 2nd, was a girl she could be seen every Sunday morning in the back of a Rolls-Royce with her grandmother, Queen Mary, going out of the gate of Buckingham Palace, around the statue of Queen Victoria and back into the Palace through the other gates. Every time she went out and back in she saluted the policemen on the gates. Her grandmother was training her to acknowledge a uniformed officer automatically and salute him. The royal birth and royal blood hadn't done away with the need for training.

In the same way we who are born children of God still need training and our lives down here on Earth are part of the training process. God wants us to live holy and self-controlled lives down here so that our rewards will come to us in the future. 'For this very reason, make every effort to add to your faith goodness; and to goodness, knowledge; and to knowledge, self-control; and to self-control, perseverance; and to perseverance, godliness;

and to godliness, brotherly kindness; and to brotherly kindness, love. For if you possess these qualities in increasing measure, they will keep you from being ineffective and unproductive in your knowledge of our Lord Jesus Christ. But if anyone does not have them, he is near-sighted and blind, and has forgotten that he has been cleansed from his past sins. Therefore, my brothers, be all the more eager to make your calling and election sure. For if you do these things, you will never fall, and *you will receive a rich welcome into the eternal kingdom* of our Lord and Saviour Jesus Christ' (2 Peter 1:5-11 NIV).

Paul's exhortation is 'to live a life worthy of the calling you have received' (Eph. 4:1 NIV).

We are the ruling aristocracy in His Eternal Kingdom and we are being trained here. The Holy Spirit – 'the Spirit of the age to come' (Heb. 6:5 NIV) – is our tutor and we must receive His training well. The degree of authority we have will depend upon how well we have responded in the lives we have led here. 'For of this you can be sure: No immoral, impure or greedy person – such a man is an idolater – has any inheritance in the kingdom of Christ and of God' (Eph. 5:5 NIV).

A diligent student will have confidence in God and with Paul he will be able to look forward to the Coming Day. I pray that we might all be able to say with him 'the time has come for my departure. I have fought the good fight, I have finished the race, I have kept the faith. Now there is in store for me the crown of righteousness, which the Lord, the righteous judge, will award to me on that day – and not only to me, but also to all who have longed for his appearing' (2 Tim. 4:6-8 NIV).

12

God's Family Today

'From one man he made every nation of men, that they should inhabit the whole earth; and he determined the times set for them and the exact places where they should live' (Acts 17:26 NIV).

Our God is the Lord of the Earth and He has determined the geography and history of every race of men. He knows the Eskimos of the frozen north and the Hottentots of the Kalahari desert; the Japanese engineeers and the Arab oil sheiks; the pygmies of the Congo and the businessmen of the City of London. Big and small, clever and dull, rich and poor, black and white – all are men and women in need of salvation and candidates, therefore, for His love. 'Whosoever shall call on the name of the Lord shall be saved' (Acts 2:21) applies to everyone, for 'God is no respecter of persons' (Acts 10:34).

The wonderful news is that from every continent, every nation and every race God has people who have called upon Jesus as Saviour and who have become His children. As a result they have become members of a new race, a new nation and a new family. 'You are no longer foreigners and aliens, but fellow-citizens with God's people and members of God's household' (Eph. 2:19 NIV).

We haven't been removed from our nations but kept among them, so that God's family, His heavenly nation, lies scattered in every race among whom they act as God's ambassadors. In God's family are people of every language and every cultural background who are ready to tell the good news of Jesus all over the world. We are God's fifth column — looking like ordinary men and women, and yet really citizens of heaven whose first allegiance is to God.

We are the 'Church of Jesus Christ – the 'called-out ones' – who, being no longer *of* the world, are nevertheless still *in* the world. Jesus said 'My prayer is not that you take them out of the world and that you protect them from the evil one. They are not of the world, even as I am not of it. Sanctify them by the truth; your word is truth. As you send me into the world, I have sent them into the world' (John 17:15-18 NIV).

It is through us that God wants to show the world that there is a Father in heaven who longs for children, and a Saviour who had died that we might all be free. The Church, collectively and individually, has an important responsibility to show forth all that God is and all that He has done, and we must be faithful in so doing if we are to 'shine like stars in the Universe' (Phil. 2:15 NIV).

If we would like to see the fulness of God's blessing manifested among us we must reckon that we are God's children, and walk accordingly. The children of God have been impoverished for too long because of plain ignorance about exactly what God has done in their lives. It is time for us to live every day in the revelation of our new family relationship. If we do not, we will be like the Galatian believers whom Paul rebuked, who had begun in the Spirit but ended in the flesh.

It happens so often. Fellowships and churches start with a group of people who are all thrilled with Jesus and excited about what God has done. Before long, however, they enter the realm of the flesh and end up relating to one another purely on human or natural terms. It happens surreptitiously at first, but soon the glory dims and the excitement vanishes. It is replaced slowly by gruding duty and gossiping cliques. The devil is behind this: he knows the glory and power of the Church and because he fears it he has to 'spike its guns' somehow. Reducing it to no more than a social club or circle of malcontents renders it impotent. We must all beware, for the devil is at work.

The Church is not a social club, it is the community of the redeemed. It is the manifestation of God's family here on Earth, and through it He wants to show forth His wonderful handiwork. It is the arena in which all the wonderful things that accompany our salvation are revealed. It *is* certainly a community of sinners, but more than that, it is a community of sinners *SAVED* by grace. It is essential, therefore, that we move on as saved individuals, and function in the reality of the new creation. After all the Church only exists because of the supernatural work of God, and as such can only be sustained in glory if every member moves in the realm of the 'new man' and constantly puts off 'the old'. Jesus has turned the water of our former life into the wine which makes our hearts rejoice. We must, therefore, leave the old water pots firmly alone.

Our first responsibility is to be obedient children. In Ephesians 6:1 Paul writes 'Children, obey your parents in the Lord, for this is right. "Honour your father and mother" – which is the first commandment with a promise – "that it may go well with you and that you may enjoy long life on the earth"' (NIV). Written primarily to the natural family group it applies equally to us. As children of God we must show our Father the honour due to His Name by praising and extolling Him, but also by obeying his commandments. Many people misuse the grace of God and the love they find in the Church by thinking that once saved they can do as they please and that other Christians will just have to put up with it. 'You've got to love me' is the threat behind which they attempt to do whatever they want. They will not escape Father's discipline.

It is because we love and obey our Father in heaven that we are motivated to live and work as unto Him. 'Slaves, obey your earthly masters in everything; and do it, not only when their eye is on you and to win their favour, but with sincerity of heart and reverence for the Lord. Whatever you do, work at it with all your heart, as working for the Lord, not for men, since you know that you will receive an inheritance from the Lord as a reward. It is the Lord Christ you are serving' (Col. 3:22-24 NIV).

Once we begin living our lives as unto the Lord, conscious of our responsibility to Him all the time, our relationship with one another will follow quite naturally. All believers are our brothers and sisters, and the Bible continually exhorts us to act with this fact in our minds. We are to feel a responsibility for them and respond to them. God commands us to love one another, for love creates coherence in God's family.

We are told to

'refresh each other'	(Romans 15:32)
'encourage each other'	(Romans 1:12 NIV)
'forgive each other'	(Eph. 4:32)
'to give to each other'	(Phil. 4:14-15)
'to teach and admonish each other'	(Col. 3:16)

and all of these follow naturally from the command to:

'love each other'	(1 Peter 4:8 NIV)

If necessary we are also told to:

'suffer together'	(1 Cor. 12:26) too.

In most churches these are neglected.

Our relationship within God's family is to be put on a higher level than any of our other relationships. 'As we have opportunity, let us do good to all people, especially to those who belong to the family of believers' (Gal. 6:10 NIV). Many of us who come from close natural families know what it is to have blessings from the family – the give-and-take, the freely provided hospitality, the caring concern and relaxing together. If that is true in our ordinary lives, it should be more so in our spiritual families. Indeed we are commanded to 'carry each other's burdens, and in this way . . . fulfil the law of Christ' (Gal. 6:2 NIV); and 'Above all, love each other deeply' (1 Peter 4:8 NIV) and 'Offer hospitality to one another without grumbling' (1 Peter 4:9 NIV).

The doors (and arms) that opened to me when I became a Christian amazed me. Most non-Christians are territorial beings who guard their own privacy diligently. It gives them independence and security, but also much loneliness. The only problem with a moat and castle walls is that while keeping the enemy out, they also keep the inhabitants in. But once a person is saved the drawbridge goes down and the portcullis is taken up.

I still owe so much to the lovely family who opened their home to me and took me away on holidays with them when I was but a year or so old in the Lord. They showed me what real Christian family relationship was like, and taught me how to enjoy myself without worldliness. I experienced with them what Acts 2:46-47 describes. 'They broke bread in their homes and ate together with glad and sincere hearts, praising God and enjoying the favour of all the people' (NIV). I don't believe this describes any religious activity, or a communion service, but a loving and caring family meeting together; so vibrant that 'the Lord added to their number daily those who were being saved' (NIV).

150

Let us beware lest we use the fellowship we have with believers in a negative way – that is to share our problems and woes only. If we do we are in danger of causing our brothers and sisters to become weary and lose heart. Nehemiah in his day noted that 'The strength of the bearers of burdens is decayed, and there is much rubbish' (Neh. 4:10). Today many people are over-stretched and really under too much pressure. If we have to burden brothers and sisters with our problems, let us also make sure we encourage them with our joys and happiness. How I agree with the writings of the non-Christian who, proving himself to be wiser in his own generation than the children of light' (Luke 16:8) said 'And let your best be for your friend. If he must know the ebb of your tide, let him know the flood also. For what is your friend that you should seek him with hours to kill? Seek him always with hours to live. For it is his to fill your need but not your emptiness. And in the sweetness of friendship let there be laughter and sharing of pleasures.'[1]

Let us remember that it is primarily Jesus who is the burden bearer. We must seek Him diligently *before* seeking out our brothers and sisters. 'Is any one of you in trouble? He *should pray*' (James 5:13 NIV). Many today don't pray, but reach for the phone immediately: they will talk to ministers, elders or to anyone available, rather than to God Himself. But James 5:13 continues 'Is any one happy? Let him sing songs of praise.'

The Bible as usual gets the balance right. 'Rejoice with those who rejoice; mourn with those who mourn'. (Romans 12:15 NIV). There is positive to be shared as well as negative.

It is a true saying that 'While we choose our friends, God chooses our neighbours' and often we will find 'difficult' brothers and sisters in our lives. We need to

1. *The Prophet*. Kahlil Gibran.

acknowledge that God loves them and is responsible for them, and that He is the One who has allowed them to come into our lives. We are warned not to withdraw from fellowship. 'Let us not give up meeting together, as some are in the habit of doing, but let us encourage one another – and all the more as you see the Day approaching' (Heb. 10:25 NIV). We have all been tempted to withdraw at times because of too many burdens or difficult personalities around us. Very often they are there to allow God to deal with areas of our lives and to bring us more deeply into Jesus. It is usually a rule that just as we reach the place where we feel we can love everyone, in comes someone to make us find an even deeper revelation of God's love. We can rejoice in God's master plan.

It was Tom Lloyd[1] who pointed out the obvious, though much overlooked fact that branches grow *in* trees and NOT *on* them. They are not separate but contain the very sap and life of the root.

When Jesus said that He is the vine and we are the branches He was promising that we would be filled with His life. For our part, we have to make sure that we constantly abide in Him so that we can be filled with the fruit of His life. This is not optional, it is essential. 'Whoever claims to live in him must walk as Jesus did' (1 John 2:6 NIV). That means that we must clothe ourselves 'with compassion, kindness, humility, gentleness and patience' (Col. 3:12 NIV). He continues 'Bear with each other and forgive whatever grievances you may have against one another. Forgive as the Lord forgave you. And over all these virtues put on love, which binds them all together in perfect unity. Let the peace of Christ rule in your hearts, since as members of one body you were

1. Minister in the Rhondda Valley, South Wales.

called to peace. And be thankful' (v13-15 NIV). This applies to us all.

Let us be thankful to God for His Family and concentrate on that which is good. I have good reason for praising God for His family. My life and the life of my family has been so enriched and broadened by all my brothers and sisters. If only I had known as a teenager that such a wonderful group of people existed! All I had seen were religious, legalistic, formal people, not the radiant, caring, relaxed people that I know in such large numbers now. God is a wonderful Father presiding over a delightful family.

We are capable of so much more than we realize. If only we knew what strength we had together and what potential was in the Body of Christ, we would be much more ready to pool our various talents and resources. I probably see this more clearly than most as I travel around Britain and Europe. It came home forcibly when visiting a town in mid-Sweden called Ånge. The Christians there had asked me to visit them but had warned me that it was 'a long way north'. As my interpreter and I prayed about this the Lord showed us that I should visit them just before I sailed home from the southern port of Gothenberg. I told them the dates and it was all arranged. All I had to do was book the air ticket from Stockholm to Ånge. The problem was that no planes fitted the schedule we had arranged. I couldn't possibly speak in Ånge on Tuesday evening and catch the ferry by 10.00 am next morning. It was a problem. The Christians in Ånge were unperturbed and certain that the dates were correct – 'Of course, you must come' they said. The train had to do.

To my amazement I was met at Ånge railway station by the station master himself – he was a lovely Christian – and he carried my bags to the Christian taxi driver's car. As we sat in the back I began to explain my problem. 'You have no problem' he kept insisting, 'you have no problem.' I made no headway at all. Only after the first meeting did one of the engine drivers in the meeting tell me that everything had been arranged. I was to trust the Lord! To my amazement the station master had arranged for me to have a sleeping compartment on a train leaving Ånge at 10.30 that night. He told me that it would be uncoupled during the night and put on other trains and that by 7.30 next morning I would be in Gothenberg. Even as I sat answering some last Bible questions in his office at 10.30 that night, I could not believe it. He was in no hurry to see me go either – he was the station master (!) and no train could leave without his permission. He assured me, therefore, that there was no rush at all.

Next morning, exactly on time, the train pulled into Gothenberg. The first person I saw at the barrier was another Christian taxi driver who whisked me away to his flat for breakfast!

Which other family has such wonderful connections? We must be determined to see to it that the fulness of the family blesses every member. It would delight our Father's heart to see us laying down our lives for one another. In a human body this is exactly what happens – it needs to happen more and more in the Body of Christ, so that instead of jealousy and petty arguments dividing us, instead of factions and cliques forming, we can flow in love one towards another. 'The body is a unit, though it is made up of many parts; and though all its parts are many, they form one body. So it is with Christ' 'If the whole body were an eye, where would the sense of hearing be? If the whole body were an ear, where would the sense of smell be? But in fact God has arranged the parts in the body, every one of them, just as he wanted them to be. If they were all one part, where would be body be? As it is, there are many parts, but one body' (1 Cor. 12:12 and 17-20 NIV). 'But God has combined the members of the Body and has given greater honour to the parts that lacked it, so that there should be no division in the body, but that its parts should have equal concern for each other. If one part suffers, every part suffers with it; if one part is honoured, every part rejoices with it' (1 Cor. 12:24-26 NIV).

Our differences are either a source of strength or a source of destruction. The Galatians were warned: 'If you keep on biting and devouring each other, watch out or you will be destroyed by each aother' (Gal. 5:15 NIV). It has happened in so many churches and fellowships. Can we imagine what it does to Father's heart? Which parent is not devastated by a split, damaged, arguing family? We need to seek God's face and see Him as Father again. Only when we have a revelation of that, will we be in a position to regard the fellow-members of the Body of Christ as our beloved brothers and sisters. Let us ask God to give us a revelation of these truths:

'So in Christ we who are many form one body, and each member belongs to all the others' (Romans 12:5 NIV).

'Be devoted to one another in brotherly love. Honour one another above yourselves' (Romans 12:10 NIV).

'Be like-minded one toward another according to Christ Jesus: That he may with one mind and one mouth glorify God, even the Father of our Lord Jesus Christ' (Romans 15:5-6).

'Accept one another, then just as Christ accepted you, in order to bring praise to God' (Romans 15:7 NIV).

Only then can we move towards one another in the sort of love to which Paul was pointing when he told the Roman Christians to 'Greet one another with a holy kiss' (Romans 16:16 NIV).

The family is of great importance to God and we must

count it precious too. What a privilege and honour it is to be a child of God and to belong to His wonderful Family. May it grow and mature, for in so doing it will surely bless the heart of our Father.

'For this reason I kneel before the Father, from whom the whole family in heaven and on earth derives its name. I pray that out of his glorious riches he may strengthen you with power through his Spirit in your inner being, so that Christ may dwell in your hearts through faith. And I pray that you, being rooted and established in love, may have power, together with all the saints, to grasp how wide and long and high and deep is the love of Christ, and to know this love that surpasses knowledge – that you may be filled to the measure of all the fulness of God. Now to him who is able to do immeasurably more than all we ask or imagine, according to his power that is at work within us, to him be glory in the church and in Christ Jesus throughout all generations for ever and ever! Amen' (Eph. 3:14-21 NIV).

Other books by the same author:

'In The Beginning'   An introduction to the Genesis account of Creation.

'Victory In Jesus'   A manual for victorious Christian living.

'Possessing The Land'   The balance between faith and works.

A complete catalogue of Bible Study tapes by Roger Price may be obtained free of charge from:

'Tapes'
30 Crescent Road
Bognor Regis
West Sussex
PO21 1QG